TIMELESS TENNESSEANS

By James A. Crutchfield

THE STRODE PUBLISHERS
HUNTSVILLE, ALABAMA 35801

DEDICATED

TO

ANDREW CRUTCHFIELD SPRINKLE,

HIMSELF A "TIMELESS TENNESSEAN."

Copyright 1984
By James A. Crutchfield
All Rights In This Book
Reserved Including The Right
To Reproduce This Book Or Parts
Thereof In Any Form—Printed In U.S.A.
Library Of Congress Catalog Number 82-062704
Standard Book Number 87397-186-8

Ben West Public Library

84-08499

920.0768 C95t
Crutchfield, James Andrew.
Timeless Tennesseans.

DISCARDED
From Nashville Public Library

The Public Library
of Nashville
and Davidson
County

KEEP DATE CARD IN BOOK
POCKET

TIMELESS TENNESSEANS

CONTENTS

84-08499
PUBLIC LIBRARY OF NASHVILLE & DAVIDSON COUNTY

PREFACE

Timeless Tennesseans is a first attempt to bring together short succinct biographies of outstanding men and women especially significant to the history of Tennessee. Some of those included were actually born in Tennessee and made their mark there; some were born in the state, but excelled somewhere else; and others were not even native-born at all, but because of some Tennessee connection, made a contribution—good or bad—to the history of the Volunteer State or elsewhere.

The reader will find soldiers, politicians, actors, scientists, artists, writers, statesmen, religious leaders, athletes, teachers, laborers, and not a few outlaws in this assemblage of profiles. However, each entry—in one way or another—sheds an interesting light on some phase of Tennessee history. The collection is by no means complete, and the author fully realizes that many people who could and should have been included within these pages were not. This was not oversight on my part, but rather an inability, because of the time factor, to collect data on all but a small percent of those eligible for inclusion.

Many authors of biographical collections such as this one rely on numerous people to assist them in the research, collection, and actual writing of the entries. In the case of *Timeless Tennesseans,* however, this was not the case. With very few exceptions, the author alone was responsible for the entries herein, and any omissions, errors, or other shortcomings in the book must be directed entirely to him.

The only profiles which were the result of the scholarship of others are those accompanied by a cross-reference to other entries. These peoples' names and biographies were supplied by Steve Eng and Ted Yeatman of Nashville, two historians who have dedicated a great deal of time to discovering the truth about some of the lesser known contributors to Tennessee history. Steve and Ted are astute researchers, and as such, have documented many Tennessee connections among such "non-Tennessee" personages as Jesse James, Francis Crawford, and Ned Buntline. My sincere thanks go to Messrs. Eng and Yeatman for their initiative and enthusiasm in documenting thése relatively unknown tidbits of Tennessee history.

I would like to thank Mrs. Marian de Monbrun McBroom, the past president of the DeMonbreum Society, for her assistance in the biography of Timothy Demonbreun, who was generally recognized as the first white man to permanently settle in the Nashville area. Thanks also to Mary Glenn Hearne, Hershel Payne, Celia Fogel, and Betsy Fisher of the Nashville Metropolitan Public Library.

Finally, I would like to thank Dave Akens, the owner of Strode Publishers, for allowing me the time required to complete this work. Mr. Akens' contributions in the local history publishing field are outstanding, and it has been a pleasure working with him and his staff.

James A. Crutchfield
Franklin, Tennessee

TIMELESS TENNESSEANS

A

ADAIR, James (1709—1783)

Born in County Antrim, Ireland; died in North Carolina. An early trader among several important Indian tribes of the southeastern United States. His book, *The History of the American Indians,* published in London in 1775, is an invaluable record of the customs and lifestyles of the Cherokee, Choctaw, and Chickasaw tribes, among others. Adair erroneously believed that the American Indians were descended from the Ten Lost Tribes of Israel.

ADAMS, John (July 1, 1825—November 30, 1864)

Born in Nashville, Tennessee; died at Franklin, Tennessee. Was graduated from West Point in 1846. Served in the Mexican War. Resigned his commission in the United States Army in 1861 and became a colonel in the Confederate Army in 1862. Was promoted to brigadier general in 1862. Was killed in the Battle of Franklin.

Miller: *Photographic History of the Civil War*

ADAMS, Robert Huntington (1792—July 2, 1832)

Born in Rockbridge County, Virginia; died in Natchez, Mississippi; buried in Natchez. Practiced law in Knoxville, Tennessee. Moved to Mississippi and was elected to the State House of Representatives in 1828. Served in the United States Senate from 1830 to 1832.

ADAMS, Stephen (October 17, 1807—May 11, 1857)

Born in the Pendleton District, South Carolina; died in Memphis, Tennessee;

buried in Memphis. Moved to Franklin County, Tennessee, as a child. Was educated and practiced law there. Served in the Tennessee Senate from 1833 to 1835. Served as a circuit judge in Mississippi. Was elected to the United States House of Representatives from Mississippi in 1845, serving until 1847. Served in the United States Senate from Mississippi in the vacancy caused by Jefferson Davis's resignation in 1852.

AGEE, James (November 27, 1909—May 16, 1955)

Born in Knoxville, Tennessee. Was graduated from Harvard University in 1932. Was on the staffs of *Fortune* magazine in 1936 and *Time* magazine from 1939 to 1943 and was the film critic for *The Nation* from 1943 to 1948. Was the author of *Let Us Now Praise Famous Men* and the screen plays for *The Quiet One* and *African Queen*. He was awarded the Pulitzer Prize for *A Death In The Family*.

AKEMAN, David "Stringbean"(June 17, 1915—November 10, 1973)

Born in Annville, Kentucky; died in Goodlettsville, Tennessee. Made his first banjo at age 12. Began playing professionally at age 18 in the Lexington, Kentucky, area. During the late 1930s, he worked with Charlie Monroe, then with Bill Monroe on the Grand Ole Opry in 1942. Akeman was an outstanding banjo player in the style of Uncle Dave Macon and appeared on network television in the "Hee Haw" series. He was tragically murdered, along with his wife, Estelle, at their home near Goodlettsville, Tennessee.

Les Leverett

ALEXANDER, Adam Rankin (November 1, 1781—November 1, 1848)

Born in Washington County, Virginia; died in Marshall County, Mississippi; buried in Marshall County. A veteran of the War of 1812, he served in both the Tennessee Senate and the Tennessee House of Representatives from 1815 to 1819 and from 1841 to 1845 respectively. Rankin was a member of the first county court of Madison County, Tennessee, and he was elected as a Federalist to the United States House of Representatives, serving from 1823 to 1827, when he was defeated by David Crockett.

ALLEN, Robert (June 19, 1778—August 19, 1844)

Born in Augusta County, Virginia; died in Carthage, Tennessee; buried in Lebanon, Tennessee. Served in the War of 1812 under Andrew Jackson. Was elected to the United States House of Representatives and served from 1819 to 1827.

ALLISON, John (1854—January 7, 1898)

Born near Clifton, Tennessee; died near Clifton; buried near Clifton. Youngest brother of the notorious Clay Allison, John followed his brother West after the War Between the States. He and his brother were involved in a gunfight at the Olympic Dance Hall in Las Animas, Colorado, on December 21, 1876. Becoming drunk and quarrelsome, they sought to pick a fight with various patrons and found trouble with a local constable named Charles Faber and two deputies. Faber shot John with a Greener 10-gauge but was killed by Clay. John survived his wounds and returned to Tennessee following the death of his brother in 1887. (See also ALLISON, Robert Clay.)

ALLISON, Robert Clay (1841—July 2, 1887)

Born in Clifton, Tennessee; died in Pecos, Texas; buried in Pecos. Clay Allison, who later became well known as a Western gunfighter and brawler, is credited with his first killing in March 1862. While home on medical leave for a condition described as "...partly epileptic and partly maniacal," he killed a corporal of the Third Illinois Cavalry who attempted to loot the Allison farm. Allison later served with Biffle's ninth Tennessee Cavalry. Following the war he moved to the Southwest, along with his two brothers and sister, and became notorious. (See also ALLISON, John.)

ANDERSON, Alexander Outlaw (November 10, 1794—May 23, 1869)

Born in Jefferson County, Tennessee; died in Knoxville, Tennessee; buried in Knoxville. Was graduated from Washington College in Greeneville, Tennessee. Served under Andrew Jackson in the War of 1812. Practiced law in Dandridge and Knoxville, Tennessee. Served in the United States Senate from 1840-1841. Led an overland party to California in 1849. Was judge of the California Supreme Court from 1851 to 1853. Later, practiced law in Mobile, Alabama.

ANDERSON, James Patton (February 12, 1822—September 1, 1873)

Born in Franklin County, Tennessee; died in Memphis, Tennessee. Fought in the Mexican War. Was a legislator in Mississippi and a United States marshall in the Washington Territory in 1853 and later was a major general in the Confederate Army.

ANDERSON, Joseph Inslee (November 5, 1757—April 14, 1837)

Born in Pennsylvania; buried in Washington, D.C. Was appointed by President George Washington as judge of the Southwest Territory, later Tennessee. Served there from 1791 to 1796. Succeeded William Blount to the United States Senate. Was appointed by President James Madison to the post of Comptroller of the United States. Anderson County, Tennessee, is named in his honor.

Temple: East Tennessee and the Civil War

ANDERSON, Josiah McNair (November 29, 1807—November 8, 1861)

Born in Dunlap, Tennessee; died in Marion County, Tennessee; buried in Sequatchie County, Tennessee. Served in both houses of the Tennessee legislature. Was speaker of the state senate from 1843 to 1845 and from 1847 to 1849. Was elected as a Whig to the United States House of Representatives, serving from 1849 to 1851. Was delegate to the Peace Conference in 1861. Was appointed a colonel in the Provisional Army of Tennessee in 1861.

ANDERSON, Samuel R. (1804-1883)

Born in Sumner County, Tennessee; died in Nashville, Tennessee. Served as a lieutenant colonel in the Mexican War. Was commissioned a major general in the Tennessee Militia on May 9, 1861. On July 9, 1861 he was made brigadier general in the Confederate Provisional Army. Commanded a brigade under General Loring.

ANDERSON, William Coleman (July 10, 1853—September 8, 1902)

Born in Greene County, Tennessee; died in Newport, Tennessee; buried in Newport. Was a graduate of Tusculum College. Studied law and was admitted to the bar in 1878. Practiced law in Newport. Was founder of the Newport newspaper, *Plain Talk*. Was county court clerk of Cocke County, Tennessee, from 1877 to 1878. Served in the Tennessee House of Representatives from 1881 to 1883. Served in the United States House of Representatives from 1895 to 1897. At his death he was mayor of Newport.

ANDREWS, Frank Maxwell (February 3, 1884—May 3, 1943)

Born in Nashville, Tennessee; died over Iceland. Was graduated from West Point in 1906. In October 1940 he became commander of the Panama Canal Air Force, and in 1941 he became the first air officer ever to hold command of an entire theater of operations when he assumed the Caribbean Defense Command. Later, he became commander of all United States Army forces in the Middle East. In 1943 he replaced General Dwight Eisenhower as commander of United States Army Forces in Europe. Andrews was killed in an airplane accident over Iceland. Andrews Air Force Base, Maryland, is named in his honor.

ANDREWS, George (December 28, 1826—August 22, 1889)

Born in Putney, Vermont. Was judge of the Tennessee Supreme Court from 1868 to 1870. Served on the Board of Trustees of the University of Tennessee and was chairman of the executive committee. Was killed in a railway accident while en route from Knoxville, Tennessee, to Middlesboro, Kentucky.

ANTHONY, Sister

See O'CONNELL, Mary.

ARMSTRONG, Robert (September 28, 1792—February 23, 1854)

Born in Abingdon, Virginia; died in Washington, D. C. Fought in the War of 1812 under Andrew Jackson. Was postmaster of Nashville from 1829 to 1835. Was appointed to the post of United States consul to Liverpool,

England, in 1845, and served in that capacity until 1849.

ARNOLD, Thomas Dickens (May 3, 1798—May 26, 1870)

Born in Spotsylvania County, Virginia; died in Jonesborough, Tennessee; buried in Greeneville, Tennessee. Taught school in Knox and Grainger counties, Tennessee. Practiced law in Knoxville. Was a member of the United States House of Representatives from 1831 to 1833, and again from 1841 to 1843. In April 1833 an attempt was made on his life on the Capitol steps in Washington, D. C.

ASBURY, Francis (August 20, 1745—May 31, 1816)

Born in Staffordshire, England; died in Spotsylvania, Virginia; buried in Baltimore, Maryland. A Methodist churchman second only to John Wesley in importance to the denomination. Organized the circuit riders, dauntless preachers who traveled hundreds of miles through all types of weather to bring the Gospel to the backwoods. Asbury was a frequent visitor to the Nashville area, which was, at the time, a hotbed of Methodist activity.

Pageant of America

ASHE, John Baptista (1810—December 29, 1857)

Born in Rocky Point, North Carolina; died in Galveston, Texas; buried in Galveston. Practiced law in Brownsville, Tennessee, after graduation from Trinity College in Hartford, Connecticut. Was elected as a Whig to the United States House of Representatives, serving from 1843 to 1845. Afterwards, he moved to Texas where he continued his law practice.

ATKINS, John De Witt Clinton (June 4, 1825—June 2, 1908)

Born in Henry County, Tennessee; died in Paris, Tennessee; buried in Paris. Served in the United States House of Representatives from 1857 to 1859, and again from 1873 to 1883. Served as the United States commissioner of Indian Affairs in President Grover Cleveland's administration. During the War Between the States, he was a representative in the Confederate Congress from 1862 to 1865.

ATKINSON, Thomas (August 6, 1807—January 4, 1881)

Born in Mansfield, Virginia; died in Wilmington, North Carolina; buried in Wilmington. Was graduated from Hampden-Sydney College in 1825 and was ordained a deacon in the Protestant Episcopal Church in 1836. Became a bishop in 1853. Was one of the founders of the University of the South at Sewanee, Tennessee.

ATTAKULLAKULLA (1700 ?—1778)

Born in North Carolina; died in Running Water Town in Tennessee. Sometimes known as the "Little Carpenter" because of his small stature. Attakullakulla was a celebrated Cherokee leader. He traveled to England with Sir Alexander Cuming in 1730. Was a devoted friend of the English until the Revolution when he raised a regiment of 500 Cherokees, which he then offered to the Americans. His father-in-law was Oconostota, his son was Dragging Canoe, and his niece was Nancy Ward, all three famous Cherokees in their own rights.

AUSTELL, Alfred (January 14, 1814—December 7, 1881)

Born in Dandridge, Tennessee; died in Atlanta, Georgia. Was an organizer and first president of the Atlanta National Bank, the first Southern institution chartered under the National Banking Act of 1863. Was chairman of the board of the Atlanta and Charlotte Air Line Railroad and a founder of Austell and Inman, the largest cotton brokerage business in the world at the time.

AVERY, William Thomas (Tecumseh) (November 11, 1819—May 22, 1880)

Born in Hardeman County, Tennessee; died in Crittenden County, Arkansas; buried in Memphis, Tennessee. Attended Old Jackson College in Columbia, Tennessee. Practiced law in Memphis. Served in the Tennessee House of Representatives from 1843 to 1845. Was elected to the United States House of Representatives as a Democrat, serving from 1857 to 1861. Was a lieutenant colonel in the Confederate Army and was captured and served time at the federal prison on Johnson's Island.

B

BACHMAN, Nathan Lynn (August 2, 1878—April 23, 1937)

Born in Chattanooga, Tennessee; died in Washington, D.C.; buried in Chattanooga. Was judge of the Tennessee Supreme Court from 1918 to 1924. Later became United States senator, succeeding Cordell Hull.

BAILEY, James Edmund (August 15, 1822—Decmeber 29, 1885)

Born in Montgomery County, Tennessee; died in Clarksville, Tennessee; buried in Clarksville. Served in the Tennessee House of Representatives from 1853 to 1855. Practiced law in Clarksville. Was a delegate to the Peace Convention in 1861. Was elected to the United States Senate in 1877 to complete Andrew Johnson's term.

BAILY, Francis (April 28, 1774—August 30, 1844)

Born in Newbury, England; died in London, England. Was a founder and four times president of the Royal Astronomical Society of Great Britain. As a young man (1796—1797) Bailey toured the United States. He traveled the entire length of the Natchez Trace, arriving in Nashville on July 31, 1797. His journal, published posthumously in 1856, contains interesting descriptions of people and places encountered in his travels.

Royal Astronomical Society

BALCH, George Beall (January 3, 1821—1908)

Born in Tennessee; died in Baltimore, Maryland. Was appointed midshipman in the United States Navy in 1837 and worked himself up through the ranks to rear admiral in 1878. Was a Mexican War veteran. Served at the United States Naval Academy from 1861 to 1862. Served at the United States Navy Yard at Washington, D.C., from 1865 to 1868. Was the superintendent of the United States Naval Academy from 1879 to 1881. Was commander in chief of the Pacific Station from 1881 to 1882.

BARKSDALE, William (August 21, 1821—July 3, 1863)

Born in Rutherford County, Tennessee; died at Gettysburg, Pennsylvania; buried in Jackson, Mississippi. Attended the University of Nashville. Practiced law in Mississippi and was the editor of the *Columbus* (Mississippi) *Democrat* in 1840. Served in the Mexican War from 1847 to 1848. Served in the United States House of Representatives from Mississippi from 1853 to 1861. Was a brigadier general in the Confederate Army. Was killed at Gettysburg.

BARNARD, Edward Emerson (December 16, 1857—February 6, 1923)

Born in Nashville, Tennessee. Learned photography as a boy and taught himself astronomy. Graduated from Vanderbilt University in 1887. Was in charge of the Vanderbilt Observatory from 1883 to 1887. Was an astronomer at the Lick Observatory in California from 1887 to 1895 and became a professor of astronomy at the University of Chicago and an assistant at the Yerkes Observatory beginning in 1895. Barnard discovered Jupiter's fifth moon in 1892; he also discovered sixteen comets, and was a pioneer in the new field of celestial photography. Many foreign scientific societies honored him.

BARRINGER, Daniel Laurens (October 1, 1788—October 16, 1852)

Born in Cabarrus County, North Carolina; died in Shelbyville, Tennessee; buried in Shelbyville. Was speaker of the Tennessee House of Representatives from 1843 to 1845. Practiced law at Shelbyville. Barringer had served in the United States House of Representatives from 1826 to 1835 while still a resident of North Carolina. He was an unsuccessful candidate for Congress from Tennessee in 1839 and was a Whig presidential elector for Henry Clay in 1844.

BARROW, Alexander (March 27, 1801—December 29, 1846)

Born near Nashville, Tennessee; died in Baltimore, Maryland; buried near Bayou Sara, Louisiana. Attended the United States Military Academy. Practiced law in Nashville before moving to Louisiana. Served in the Louisiana House of Representatives and was a United States senator from 1841 until his death.

BARROW, George Washington (October 5, 1807—October 19, 1866)

Born in Davidson County, Tennessee; died in St. Louis, Missouri; buried in Nashville. Was educated at Davidson Academy in Nashville. Practiced law in

Nashville and was editor of the Nashville *Republican-Banner*. Served in the Tennessee House of Representatives from 1837 to 1839 and in the Tennessee Senate from 1861 to 1862. Was appointed United States charge d'affaires at Lisbon, Portugal, in 1841 and served until 1844. Served in the United States House of Representatives from 1847 to 1849.

BARTON, David (December 14, 1783—September 28, 1837)

Born in Greeneville, Tennessee; died in Boonville, Missouri; buried in Boonville. Spent most of his life in Missouri, where he was a deputy attorney general for the territory, a circuit judge, and the speaker of the Missouri territorial legislature. Served in the United States Senate from 1821 to 1831.

BASKERVILLE, William Malone (February 1, 1888—May 18, 1953)

Born in Nashville, Tennessee; died in Baltimore, Maryland. Was educated at Vanderbilt University and the University of the South. Began his career as a reporter on the *Nashville Tennessean* in 1907. Was later associated with the *Commercial Appeal,* the *Montgomery Advisor,* and the *New York Journal.* Became the news editor of the Associated Press in 1911. Was the managing editor for the *Atlanta Georgian-American* from 1922 to 1926. Was elected to the board of directors of Hearst Consolidated Publishing in 1938.

BASS, John Meredith (October 23, 1845—1908)

Born in Nashville, Tennessee; died in Nashville. Was graduated from Bethany College in West Virginia. Received his law degree from Cumberland University at Lebanon, Tennessee. Was the secretary-treasurer of the University of Nashville, beginning in 1894. Was the secretary of the Tennessee Historical Society for 12 years. Served on the board of directors of Watkins Institute in Nashville for four years. Was a writer of historical articles and papers and co-editor of the *American Historical Magazine.*

BATE, William Brimage (1826—March 9, 1905)

Born in Sumner County, Tennessee; died in Washington, D.C.; buried in Nashville, Tennessee. Governor of Tennessee from 1883 to 1887. Was a brigadier general in the Confederate Army. After the War Between the States, Bate returned to his farm in Sumner

County and his law practice in Nashville. As governor, he retired the state debt that had harrassed officials for years. Later, he was elected to the United States Senate, where he served until his death.

BATES, Finis L. (August 22, 1848—November 29, 1923)

Born in Guntown, Mississippi; buried in Memphis, Tennessee. Studied law under Senator J. Z. George; served as city attorney of Greenville, Mississippi; became law partner of Senator Leroy Percy, and settled in Memphis. In Texas in the 1870s Bates met a man who claimed to be Lincoln's assassin, John Wilkes Booth. Again in 1903 he identified the body of a suicide, David E. George, as really being Booth. He had George's body embalmed, and its mummified remains were stored for years in Bates' Memphis garage. His Memphis-published *The Escape and Suicide of John Wilkes Booth* (1907) sold 70,000 copies, and the mummy became a carnival side-show exhibit years after Bates's death. In the 1970s Bates's story was defended frequently on East Coast talk shows and in *Rolling Stone*, by Nathaniel Orlowek. (See BOOTH, John Wilkes; GEORGE, David E.)

BATTLE, Joel Allen (September 19, 1811—August 20, 1872)

Born in Davidson County, Tennessee; died in Davidson County; buried in Davidson County. Was owner of the City Hotel in Nashville in 1869. Was superintendent of the state prison in 1872. Earlier, was appointed but did not serve as state treasurer during the War Between the States. Served in the Seminole War and in the Confederate Army. Was captured at Ft. Donelson.

BAXTER, Edmund Dillabunty (August 28, 1838—1910)

Born in Nashville, Tennessee; died in Nashville. Was admitted to the bar in 1857. Practiced law in Nashville for all of his life. Was a professor of law at Vanderbilt University from 1875 to 1905. Was a delegate to the Universal Congress of Lawyers and Jurists held in St. Louis in 1904.

BAXTER, Jere (February 11, 1852—1904)

Born in Nashville, Tennessee. Was educated locally at Montgomery Bell Academy. Was a lawyer and the publisher of the *Legal Reporter*. Prior to age 30 he became the president of the Memphis and Charlotte Railroad. Was responsible for the building of the city of Sheffield, Alabama. Was a candidate for governor of Tennessee in 1889. Was the organizer and president of the Tennessee Central Railroad.

BAXTER, John (March 5, 1819—April 2, 1886)

Born in North Carolina. Served in the North Carolina legislature. Moved to Tennessee where he edited the Knoxville *Daily Chronicle* from 1862 to 1867. Was a member of the 1870 Constitutional Convention. Served as a United States circuit judge from 1877 to 1886.

BEALL, John Yates (January 1, 1835—February 24, 1865)

Born in Jefferson County, Virginia; died at Ft. Lafayette, New York; buried in Jefferson County, Virginia. Was the fiance of Martha O'Bryan of Franklin, Tennessee. Beall was executed in New York by federal authorities, after conviction of espionage. Miss O'Bryan never married but devoted her life to others. The Martha O'Bryan Community Center in Nashville is named in her honor.

BEAN, Lydia

See BEAN, William.

BEAN, Russell (1769—1839)

Born in Washington County, Tennessee. Was the first white child to be born in the region later to become Tennessee. Was the son of William and Lydia Bean. The site of his birthplace, along the Watauga River in Washington County, is now covered by Boone Lake. In adult life Bean was a gunsmith by profession.

BEAN, William

William Bean and his wife, Lydia, were the first permanent settlers in the territory which eventually became Tennessee. Early in 1769 the couple built a cabin near the Watauga River. Their child, Russell, was born there, becoming the first white child to be born in Tennessee. The site of the cabin is now covered by Boone Lake.

BEARD, Richard (1799—December 2, 1880)

Born in Sumner County, Tennessee; died in Lebanon, Tennessee. Was a circuit rider in 1820. Taught at Cumberland College in Princeton, Kentucky, where he served as president from 1843 to 1854. Was professor of theology at Cumberland University at Lebanon, Tennessee. Was the author of *Lectures on Theology* and *Miscellaneous Sermons, Reviews, and Essays*.

BEARD, W. D. (October 28, 1835—December 7, 1910)

Born in Princeton, Kentucky; died in Nashville, Tennessee; buried in Memphis, Tennnessee. Was a judge of the Tennessee Supreme Court in 1890 and again from 1894 to 1910. Was chief justice from 1902 to 1910. During the War Between the States, he served on the staff of General A. P. Stewart.

BELL, Bennett Douglas (July 4, 1852—August 12, 1934)

Born in Sumner County, Tennessee. Was judge of the Tennessee Supreme Court from 1908 to 1910. Practiced law in Gallatin, Tennessee, and Nashville. Held extensive lands in Sumner and Davidson counties, Tennessee.

BELL, John (February 18, 1796—September 11, 1869)

Born in Davidson County, Tennessee; died in Stewart County, Tennessee; buried in Nashville, Tennessee. Served in the Tennessee Senate from 1817 to 1819 and in the Tennessee House of Representatives from 1847 to 1849. Practiced law in Franklin, Murfreesboro, and Nashville, Tennessee. Served in the United States House of Representatives from 1827 to 1841; was speaker in 1834. Was United States secretary of war in 1841. Served in the United States Senate from 1847 to 1859. Was unsuccessful candidate for president of the United States in 1860 against Abraham Lincoln and Stephen Douglas.

Harper's Pictorial History of the Civil War

BELL, Montgomery (January 3, 1769—April 1, 1855)

Born in Chester County, Pennsylvania; died in Dickson (now Cheatham) County, Tennessee; buried in Cheatham County. Migrated to Tennessee as a young man and established several iron smelters in Dickson County. Was builder of the tunnel through the Narrows of the Harpeth River, now in Cheatham County. Upon his

Corlew: A History of Dickson County

death, Bell left a large amount of money for the establishment of the Montgomery Bell Academy in Nashville.

BELL, Tyree H. (September 6, 1815—August 30, 1902)

Born in Cincinnati, Ohio; died in New Orleans, Louisiana; buried in Fresno County, California. As a child, moved to Sumner County, Tennessee, where he was raised and received his education. Was a farmer and stock raiser. Served in the Confederate Army as a captain all the way through the ranks to brigadier general and saw action at Belmont and at Shiloh. Moved to California in 1875.

BENTEEN, Frederick William (August 24, 1834—June 22, 1898)

Born in Petersburg, Virginia; died in Atlanta, Georgia; buried in Arlington, Virginia. Captain Benteen was in command of H Troop, seventh United States Cavalry, stationed at Ash Barracks, in North Nashville, Tennessee, from June 1, 1871, to March 10, 1873. During this period, H Troop was engaged in activities against the Night Riders in Alabama and Mississippi and illegal distilleries. Benteen was later to play a major role in the Battle of the Little Big Horn, June 25-27, 1876, as commander of a battalion of the seventh Cavalry. He retired as a brevet brigadier general in 1890. (See also DE RUDIO, Charles Camilus; GIBSON, Francis Marion; and WINDOLPH, Charles.)

BENTON, Thomas Hart (March 14, 1782—April 10, 1858)

Born in Orange County, North Carolina; died in Washington, D. C.; buried in St. Louis, Missouri. Practiced law in Franklin, Tennessee, as a young man. Served in the Tennessee Senate from 1809 to 1811. A gunfight with Andrew Jackson on the public square in Nashville in 1813 caused Benton to move to Missouri, where he was elected to the United States Senate in 1821. He was the first person to serve thirty consecutive years in the Senate. He also served as a United States representative from Missouri from 1853 to 1855.

BENTON, Thomas Hart (September 5, 1816—April 10, 1879)

Born in Williamson County, Tennessee; died in St. Louis, Missouri; buried in Marshalltown, Iowa. Conducted the first classical school in Iowa in 1838. Was a member of the first Iowa Senate from 1846 to 1848. Was a brigadier general in the United States Army during the War Between the States.

BERTINATTI, Countess Eugenie (September 6, 1826—December 9, 1906)

Born near Castalian Springs, Tennessee; died in Nashville, Tennessee; buried in Washington, D.C. Was first married to Council Rogers Bass, a Mississippi planter. After his death, she married the Italian ambassador to the United States, Chevalier Bertinatti. Lived in Italy and represented, with her husband, her adopted country in Turkey and in several courts in Europe. After his death she kept her residence in Italy and died in Nashville while visiting.

Cisco: Historic Sumner County, Tennessee

BIERCE, Ambrose (June 24, 1842—1914?)

Born in Meigs County, Ohio. The self-educated Bierce volunteered for the Union cause in 1861. He was a reconnaissance scout under General Hazen through the mid-Tennessee and Chattanooga campaigns. His Civil War sojourn in Tennessee resulted in such short stories as "A Baffled Ambuscade," "The Story of a Conscience," "George Thursont," "The Major's Tale," and "A Resumed Identity." Generally, Bierce's war tales are among the world's best and probably the first to desentimentalize the topic.

Tennessee Western History and Folklore Society

Bierce was later a famous San Francisco wit and literary mentor, and his best fiction and epigrams are immortal. He disappeared mysteriously, seeking to meet Mexican revolutionary Pancho Villa.

BLACKBURN, Gideon (August 27, 1772—August 23, 1838)

Born in Augusta County, Virginia; died in Carlinville, Illinois. Was an early preacher and educator. Was the first headmaster of Harpeth Academy in Franklin, Tennessee (1811). Organized the Franklin Presbyterian Church in 1811 and the First Presbyterian Church in Nashville, Tennessee, in 1814.

BLACKMORE, George Dawson (February 1762—September 27, 1833)

Born near Hagerstown, Maryland; died in Sumner County, Tennessee. Was a veteran of the Revolutionary War. Moved to Sumner County, Tennessee, with the Bledsoes or shortly afterwards. Was active in defending the Cumberland Settlements from the Indians. After the Indian wars, he settled on a farm four miles from Gallatin, Tennessee. Was prominent in Virginia before coming to Tennessee. Once had a fort in Scott County, Tennessee.

BLACKWELL, Julius W.

Born in Virginia. Moved to Tennessee and became a member of the United States House of Representatives from 1839 to 1841 and from 1843 to 1845. By party, he was a Van Buren Democrat. Blackwell lived in Athens, Tennessee.

BLAIR, JOHN III (August 13, 1790—July 9, 1863)

Born near Jonesborough, Tennessee; died in Jonesborough; buried in Jonesborough. Practiced law in Washington County, Tennessee. Served in the Tennessee Senate in 1819 and 1820 and from 1821 to 1823. Served as a Democrat in the United States House of Representatives from 1823 to 1835. Was elected to the Tennessee House of Representatives and served from 1849 to 1851.

BLEDSOE, Anthony (1733—July 20, 1788)

Born in Culpeper County, Virginia; died in Castalian Springs, Tennessee; buried in Castalian Springs. Was an early settler of the Cumberland Valley. Built a station at Bledsoe's Lick (Castalian Springs) in Sumner County, Tennessee. Was a surveyor by profession. Served in a number of official capacities in the Cumberland Settlements. Was killed by Indians in an attack upon his station.

BLEDSOE, Isaac (1735—April 9, 1793)

Born in Culpeper County, Virginia; died in Castalian Springs, Tennessee;

buried in Castalian Springs. Was an early settler of the Cumberland Valley. With his brother, Anthony, he established a station at Bledsoe's Lick (Castalian Springs) in Sumner County, Tennessee. Like his brother, Bledsoe was an important figure in the community, and also like his brother, he was killed by Indians while defending his station.

BLOUNT, William (March 26, 1749—March 21, 1800)

Born in North Carolina; buried in Knoxville, Tennessee. Was the first and only governor of the Territory of the United States, South of the River Ohio, the region which later became Tennessee. Served in this role from 1790 to 1796. He selected Rocky Mount as the territory's first capital, but later moved it to Knoxville. Today's University of Tennessee was originally named Blount College in his honor. He later became a United States senator from Tennessee but was removed from office on conspiracy charges.

Temple: East Tennessee and the Civil War

BLOUNT, William Grainger (1784—May 21, 1827)

Born in Craven County, North Carolina; died in Paris, Tennessee; buried in Paris. Practiced law in Knoxville, Tennessee. Served in the Tennessee House of Representatives in 1811, became secretary of state that same year and served until 1815. Was a member of the United States House of Representatives from 1815 to 1819. Practiced law in Paris, Tennessee, in later life.

BLOUNT, Willie (April 18, 1768—September 10, 1835)

Born in Bertie County, North Carolina; died near Nashville, Tennessee; buried in Clarksville, Tennessee. Was governor of Tennessee from 1809 to 1815. Blount was a half-brother of William Blount, the governor of the Southwest Territory. Was responsible for the raising of money and troops which assured Andrew Jackson's success

Green: Lives of the Judges of the Supreme Court of Tennessee

at the Battle of New Orleans during the War of 1812.

BONTEMPS, Arna Wendell (October 13, 1902—June 4, 1973)

Born in Alexandria, Louisiana; died in Nashville, Tennessee. Attended San Fernando Academy in California from 1917 to 1920. Received a degree from Pacific Union College in 1923; received a master's degree from the University of Chicago in 1943. Was librarian at Fisk University in Nashville, Tennessee, from 1943 to 1965. Was a professor at the University of Illinois from 1966 to 1969. Lectured at Yale University from 1969 to 1973. Was the author of *Story of the Negro, Story of George Washington Carver,* and *One Hundred Years of Negro Freedom.*

BOONE, Andrew Rechmond (April 4, 1831—January 26, 1886)

Born in Davidson County, Tennessee; died in Mayfield, Kentucky; buried in Mayfield. Was a lawyer by profession. Practiced in Mayfield, Kentucky. Served as a judge in Kentucky in 1854 and again from 1858 to 1861. Was a member of the United States House of Representatives from Kentucky from 1875 to 1879.

BOONE, Daniel (November 2, 1734—September 26, 1820)

Born in Oley Township, Pennsylvania; died in Missouri; buried in Frankfort, Kentucky. An early resident of the Watauga Settlements in what later became the state of Tennessee. Was hired by Richard Henderson to clear a road from Watauga into Kentucky as part of Henderson's Transylvania Company settlement plan. While claimed by Kentucky, Boone played a large role in the early exploration and settlement of Tennessee as well.

BOONE, Hugh Craig Daniel (1898—September 12, 1981)

Born in Booneville, Tennessee; died in Nashville, Tennessee; buried in Nashville. Was a graduate of the University of Tennessee and the Cumberland University Law School in Lebanon, Tennessee. Was the night general sessions judge in Nashville, Tennessee, for years. Was a direct descendant of Daniel Boone, the frontiersman.

BOOTH, John Wilkes (May 10, 1838—April 26, 1865)

Born in Harmon County, Maryland; buried in Washington, D.C. A famous actor, Booth was overshadowed by his brilliant brother Edwin, but immortalized himself in infamy as Lincoln's assassin. At the Nashville Theater (formerly the Adelphi), Booth appeared February 1-6, 1864, in such roles as Cardinal Richelieu, Hamlet, Richard III, and others. In legend if not in fact, Booth "returned" to Tennessee in 1903 in ghoulish mummified form. One David E. George (possibly "John St. Helen") had committed suicide in Oklahoma but not before "confessing" to being the clandestinely surviving John Wilkes Booth. His mummified remains were stored in Memphis by attorney Finis L. Bates, whose *The Escape and Suicide of John Wilkes Booth* (1907) was a success. The "Booth" cadaver later became a notorious national side-show attraction. (See BATES, Finis L.; GEORGE, David E.)

BOWEN, John Henry (September 1780—September 25, 1822)

Born in Washington County, Virginia; died in Gallatin, Tennessee. Attended schools in Lexington, Kentucky. Moved to Gallatin, Tennessee, where he practiced law. Served in the United States House of Representatives as a Democrat from 1813 to 1815.

BOWIE, James (1796—March 6, 1836)

Born in Sumner County, Tennessee; died at the Alamo, Texas. Moved to Louisiana in 1802. With his brother, Reason, he owned a large sugar plantation, the first in Louisiana to use steam power to grind sugar cane. His brother Reason, not James, invented the Bowie knife. When his family was wiped out by cholera in 1834, James Bowie went to Texas where he died defending the Alamo.

BOYD, Lynn (November 22, 1800—December 17, 1859)

Born in Nashville, Tennessee; died in Paducah, Kentucky; buried in Paducah. Was instrumental in securing what is now west Tennessee from the Chickasaw Indians. Served in the Kentucky House of Representatives from 1827 to 1832 and in the United States House of Representatives from 1835 to 1837 and again from 1839 to 1855. Was speaker of the United States House from 1851 to 1855. Was elected lieutenant governor of Kentucky in 1859 but died before assuming office.

BOYD, Sempronius Hamilton (May 28, 1828—June 22, 1894)

Born near Nashville, Tennessee; died in Springfield, Missouri; buried in Springfield. Studied law in Nashville, Tennessee, then moved to Missouri in 1840, and finally to California in 1849, where he prospected for gold. Returned to Missouri in 1854 and practiced law in Springfield. Became mayor of Springfield in 1856 and was a member of the United States House of Representatives from 1863 to 1865 and again from 1869 to 1871. Was an executive for the Southwest Pacific Railroad from 1867 to 1874. Was appointed to the post of consul general of Siam in 1890 and served two years.

BOYLE, Virginia Frazer (?—December 13, 1938)

Born near Chattanooga, Tennessee; died in Memphis, Tennessee. The special office of "Poet Laureate" was created for her by the United Confederate Veterans in 1910. Was the author of *The Other Side* and *Christ in the Argonne*, among others.

BRABSON, Reese Bowen (September 16, 1817—August 16, 1863)

Born near Knoxville, Tennessee; died in Chattanooga, Tennessee; buried in Chattanooga. Practiced law in Chattanooga, Tennessee. Served in the Tennessee House of Representatives from 1851 to 1853. Was elected to the United States House of Representatives in 1859 and served until 1861. Was pro-Union during the War Between the States and did not run for reelection in 1861.

BRADEN, John (August 18, 1826—1900)

Born in New York; died in Nashville, Tennessee. Was graduated from Ohio Wesleyan University in 1853. Received a D.D. degree from Iowa University in 1873. Was the president of Central Tennessee College beginning in 1869.

BRADFORD, Joseph

See HUNTER, William Randolph.

BRADLEY, Frank Howe (September 20, 1838—March 27, 1879)

Born in New Haven, Connecticut; died near Nacooche, Georgia. Was graduated from Yale University in 1863. Was a geologist by profession, discovering a new species of *trilobite* in New York in 1857. Was professor of geology and mineralogy at the University of Tennessee from 1869 to 1875. Was killed in a mining accident in Georgia.

BREAZELLE, John Will M. (?—1861)

Born in Roane County, Tennessee (?); buried in Jasper, Tennessee. Was a lawyer by profession. Was editor of the *Tennessee Journal*. His important book, *Life As It Is*, is a valuable record of Tennessee's early history. Served in the Tennessee House of Representatives from 1829 to 1831.

BRIDGES, George Washington (October 9, 1825—March 16, 1873)

Born in Charleston, Tennessee; died in Athens, Tennessee; buried in Athens. Practiced law in Athens, Tennessee. Was attorney general of Tennessee from 1849 to 1860. Raised the Tenth Regiment of Tennessee Cavalry for the United States Army during the War Between the States. Was elected to the United States House of Representatives but was confined under arrest in Tennessee for a year, finally serving in his post from February 25 to March 3, 1863. Was circuit judge for the Fourth Judicial District of Tennessee in 1866.

BRIGHT, Aaron D. (August 10, 1838—September 11, 1898)

Born in Hinds County, Mississippi; died in Brownsville, Tennessee; buried in Brownsville. Was judge of the Tennessee Supreme Court for a short time in 1894. Previously was a captain in the Army of Northern Virginia and a lawyer.

BRIGHT, John Morgan (January 20, 1817—October 2, 1911)

Born in Fayetteville, Tennessee; died in Fayetteville; buried in Fayetteville. Educated at the University of Nashville and at Transylvania University. Practiced law in Fayetteville. Served in the Tennessee House of Representatives as a Democrat from 1847 to 1849. Was elected to the United States House of Representatives in 1871 and served until 1881. When the War Between the States broke out, he was appointed inspector general of Tennessee. Was the author of numerous newspaper articles on Lincoln County (Tennessee) history.

BROWN, Aaron Venable (August 15, 1795—March 8, 1859)

Born in Brunswick County, Virginia; died in Washington, D.C.; buried in Nashville, Tennessee. Was governor of Tennessee from 1845 to 1847. Was a lawyer by profession. Served as both a state representative and a state senator, as well as postmaster-general of the United States in President Buchanan's administration. It was during Brown's governorship that he asked for 2,600 volunteers for the upcoming Mexican conflict, and more than 30,000 responded.

BROWN, Foster Vincent (December 24, 1854—?)

Born in White County, Tennessee; died in Chattanooga, Tennessee. Was graduated from Burnett College in Tennessee in 1871. Received his law degree from Cumberland University in Lebanon, Tennessee, in 1873. Was the attorney-general of the Fourth Judicial District from 1886 to 1894. Served in the United States House of Representatives from 1895 to 1897.

BROWN, John Calvin (1827—August, 1889)

Born in Giles County, Tennessee; died in Macon County, Tennessee; buried in Pulaski, Tennessee. Was governor of Tennessee from 1871 to 1875. John Brown was former Tennessee governor Neill Brown's younger brother. Fought with the South during the War Between the States. In 1870 became the president of the constitutional convention which framed a new constitution for Tennessee. Inheriting severe monetary problems as governor, he reduced the state debt dramatically and instituted the first public school system in Tennessee.

BROWN, Milton (February 28, 1804—May 15, 1883)

Born in Lebanon, Ohio; died in Jackson, Tennessee; buried in Jackson. Practiced law in both Jackson and Paris, Tennessee. Was judge of the Chancery Court of West Tennessee from 1835 to 1841. Served in the United States House of Representatives as a Whig from 1841 to 1847. Was a founder of both Southwestern University (later Union University) and Lambuth College in Jackson, Tennessee. Was president of the Mississippi Central and Tennessee Railroad from 1854 to 1856 and of the Mobile and Ohio Railroad from 1856 to 1871.

BROWN, Neill Smith (April 18, 1810—January 30, 1886)

Born in Giles County, Tennessee; died in Nashville, Tennessee; buried in Nashville. Was governor of Tennessee from 1847 to 1849. Was a veteran of the Seminole War, a state legislator, and an attorney before he became governor. Was appointed to the post of minister to Russia by President Zachary Taylor, a position he held for three years. Was a Confederate sympathizer during the War Between the States but took no active part in the conflict.

BROWN, William Little (August 9, 1789—February 28, 1830)

Born in Cheraw, South Carolina. Was judge of the Tennessee Supreme Court of Errors and Appeals from 1822 to 1824. Served in the Tennessee

State Senate and was solicitor general of Tennessee.

BROWNING, Gordon (1895—May 23, 1976)

Born in Carroll County, Tennessee; buried in Huntingdon, Tennessee. Was governor of Tennessee from 1937 to 1939 and from 1949 to 1953. Was a decorated soldier in World War I. Practiced law after the war. Served in the United States House of Representatives for six terms where he was an opponent to President Franklin Roosevelt's radical policies. Was elected as governor with the backing of Memphis political boss Ed Crump. Later had a falling out with Crump and was responsible for the Memphian's downfall.

BROWNLOW, Walter Preston (1851—1910)

Born in Abingdon, Virginia; died in Jonesboro, Tennessee. Was the owner and editor of the *Herald and Tribune* at Jonesboro. Was the postmaster of Jonesboro in 1881. Was the doorkeeper of the Forty-Seventh Congress of the United States from 1881 to 1883 and served in the United States House of Representatives from 1897 to 1911.

BROWNLOW, William Gannaway (August 29, 1805—April 29, 1877)

Born in Wythe County, Virginia; died in Knoxville, Tennessee; buried in Knoxville. Was governor of Tennessee from 1865 to 1869, but was elected under questionable conditions. The void left in the governor's chair by Andrew Johnson's election as vice-president of the United States and the carpetbagging influences throughout the state at the end of the War created a situation whereby Brownlow was "elected" governor, but in an election in which most of the state's Confederate sympathizers were disenfranchised and unable to vote. He resigned the governorship to serve in the United States Senate.

BRYAN, Henry H. (?—May 7, 1835)

Born in Martin County, North Carolina; died in Montgomery County, Tennessee. Attended schools in North Carolina. Moved to Tennessee where he held several local offices. Was elected to the United States House of Representatives in 1819 and served until 1821.

BUCHANAN, Arthur S. (1856—December 25, 1919)

Born in DeSoto County, Mississippi; died in Memphis, Tennessee. Was judge of the Tennessee Supreme Court from 1910 to 1917. Previously practiced law in Hernando, Mississippi, and in Memphis. Served one term in the Mississippi legislature.

BUCHANAN, John Price (1847—May 14, 1930)

Born in Williamson County, Tennessee; died in Murfreesboro, Tennessee; buried in Murfreesboro. Was a farmer. Served in the Tennessee House of Representatives from 1887 to 1891. Was governor of Tennessee from 1891 to 1893. Was the first president of the State Farmers Alliance in 1888.

BUGG, Robert Malone (January 20, 1805—February 18, 1887)

Born in Boydton, Virginia; died in Lynnville, Tennessee; buried near Lynnville. Taught school in Williamson County, Tennessee before moving to Giles County, Tennessee. Was a member of the Tennessee House of Representatives from 1851 to 1853. Was elected as a Whig to the United States House of Representatives, serving from 1853 to 1855. Returned to Tennessee where he was elected to the Tennessee Senate in 1871, serving until 1873.

BUNCH, Samuel (December 4, 1786—September 5, 1849)

Born in Grainger County, Tennessee; died near Rutledge, Tennessee; buried near Rutledge. Served in the Creek War and in the War of 1812. Was a member of the Tennessee Senate from 1819 to 1825. Served in the United States House of Representatives from 1833 to 1837.

BUNTLINE, Ned

See JUDSON, Edward Zane Carroll.

BURNETT, Peter Hardeman (November 15, 1807—1895)

Born in Nashville, Tennessee; died in California; buried in Santa Clara, California. Was the first American governor of California. In earlier days he served in a judicial post in Oregon Territory, and after his governorship was appointed to the California Supreme Court. As a young man he was the leader of the first and largest immigrant wagon train ever to cross America.

BURR, Aaron (February 6, 1756—September 14, 1836)

Born in Newark, New Jersey; died in New York; buried in Princeton, New Jersey. Was vice-president of the United States under Thomas Jefferson. Made several trips to Nashville as a friend of Andrew Jackson. Was implicated in a treason scheme which since has been proven to have been the design of General James Wilkinson, rather than his own. Burr was hung in effigy on the Nashville Public Square on January 3, 1807.

BUTLER, Barbara Coggin

See COGGIN, Barbara.

BUTLER, Roderick Random (April 8, 1827—August 18, 1902)

Born in Wytheville, Virginia; died in Mountain City, Tennessee; buried in Mountain City. Served in the Tennessee House of Representatives from 1859 to 1863 and from 1879 to 1887. Served in the Tennessee Senate from 1865 to 1867 and from 1895 to 1902. Served in the United States House of Representatives from 1868 to 1875 and from 1887 to 1889. Was chairman of the first Republican State Executive Committee.

BYRNS, Joseph Wellington (July 20, 1869—June 4, 1936)

Born in Cedar Hill, Tennessee; died in Washington, D.C.; buried in Nashville, Tennessee. Served in the Tennessee House of Representatives from 1895 to 1901; was speaker from 1899 to 1901. Served in the Tennessee Senate from 1901 to 1903. Was elected to the United States House of Representatives in 1909 and served there until his death in 1936. Was speaker of the United States House during his last session. President Franklin D. Roosevelt attended his funeral in Nashville.

C

CAGE, Harry (?—1859)

Born in Sumner County, Tennessee; died in New Orleans, Louisiana; buried in Wilkinson County, Mississippi. Moved to Mississippi at an early age. Practiced law in Woodville, Mississippi. Was a judge on the Mississippi Supreme Court from 1829 to 1832 and served in the United States House of Representatives from Mississippi from 1833 to 1835.

CAGE, William (1745—March 12, 1811)

Born in Virginia; died in Sumner County, Tennessee; buried in Sumner County. Moved from Virginia to North Carolina at an early age. Served in the Revolutionary War as a major. Moved to what is now Tennessee (Sullivan County). Was the speaker of the first assembly of the State of Franklin. Was the first treasurer of the State of Franklin. Was a sheriff in the Territorial Government. Established the community at Cage's Bend in Sumner County, Tennessee.

CALDWELL, Joshua William (February 3, 1856—1909)

Born in Athens, Tennessee; died in Knoxville, Tennessee. Was graduated from the University of Tennessee in 1875 and was admitted to the bar in 1877. Was a trustee for the State Deaf and Dumb School and a lecturer on Tennessee laws and the constitutional history of the state at the University of Tennessee. Was the author of *Constitutional History of Tennessee* and *Bench and Bar of Tennessee.*

CALDWELL, Robert Porter (December 16, 1821—March 12, 1885)

Born in Adair County, Kentucky; died in Trenton, Tennessee; buried in Trenton. Studied law in Obion County, Tennessee and at Cumberland University at Lebanon, Tennessee. Served in the Tennessee House of Representatives from 1847 to 1849. Served in the Tennessee Senate from 1855 to 1857. Served in the Confederate Army under General Forrest. Was elected to the United States House of Representatives and served from 1871 to 1873.

CALDWELL, Waller C. (May 14, 1849—December 23, 1924)

Born in Obion County, Tennessee; died in Florida. Was a graduate of

Cumberland University at Lebanon, Tennessee. Was a judge of the Tennessee Supreme Court from 1886 to 1902. Retired from the bench to practice law in Trenton, Tennessee.

CALDWELL, William Parker (November 8, 1832—June 7, 1903)

Born in Carroll County, Tennessee; died in Weakley County, Tennessee; buried in Weakley County. Studied law at Cumberland University at Lebanon, Tennessee. Practiced law at Dresden and Union City, Tennessee. Served in the Tennessee House of Representatives from 1857 to 1859 and again from 1869 to 1871. Served in the United States House of Representatives from 1875 to 1879. Served in the United States Senate from 1895 to 1897.

CAMPBELL, Alexander (September 12, 1786—March 4, 1866)

Born in County Antrim, Ireland; died in Bethany, West Virginia. Attended the University of Glasgow, Scotland. Came to America in 1809. Founded the Disciples of Christ in 1827. He visited Tennessee often and by 1864 his denomination counted 350,000 members.

Pageant of America

CAMPBELL, Brookins (1808—December 25, 1853)

Born in Washington County, Tennessee; died in Washington, D.C.; buried in Greene County, Tennessee. Graduated from Washington College. Was a lawyer by profession. Was a Mexican War veteran. Was a member of the Tennessee House of Representatives from 1835 to 1839, from 1841 to 1846, and from 1851 to 1853. Was speaker of the house in 1845. Was sent to United States House in 1853 and died in office.

CAMPBELL, David (1750—1812)

Born in Augusta County, Virginia; died in Mississippi Territory. Was elected to the Tennessee Superior Court as a judge in 1797. Had previously served as a judge in North Carolina, the State of Franklin, and the Southwest Territory. Campbell was impeached in 1803, but was acquitted by the senate. In 1811, he was appointed judge for the Mississippi Territory by the president of the United States, but did not serve.

CAMPBELL, Francis J. (1832—1912)

Born in Franklin County, Tennessee. An accident blinded him at age 3½, and he did not attend school in his early years because of the lack of facilities. As a young teenager he came to Nashville to attend the newly established school for the blind. He learned the Braille system in 45 minutes and was the highest in his class upon graduation. Became an instructor and assistant superintendent for the Perkins Institute for the Blind in Boston, Massachusetts. Was a co-founder of the Royal Normal College for the Blind in England. In 1909, he was knighted by King Edward VII. He was the only blind man ever to ascend Mt. Blanc, the highest peak in the Alps.

CAMPBELL, George Washington (February 9, 1769—February 17, 1848)

Born in Sutherlandshire, Scotland; died in Nashville, Tennessee; buried in Nashville. Served as a United States congressman from 1803 to 1809. Was a judge of the Tennessee Superior Court and of its successor, the Supreme Court of Errors and Appeals from 1809 to 1811. Was United States senator from 1811 to 1815. Was secretary of the treasury in President James Madison's cabinet. Also served as the minister to Russia. Campbell sold to the city of Nashville the property upon which the State Capitol stands.

CAMPBELL, Thomas Jefferson (February 22, 1793—April 13, 1850)

Born in Jefferson County, Tennessee; died in Washington, D.C.; buried in Calhoun, Tennessee. Practiced law in Rhea County, Tennessee. Was clerk of the Tennessee House of Representatives from 1817 to 1822 and again from 1825 to 1832. Served as a member of the Tennessee House of Representatives from 1833 to 1837. Served in the United States House of Representatives from 1841 to 1843. Was clerk of the United States House of Representatives from 1847 until his death.

CAMPBELL, William Bowen (February 1, 1807—August 19, 1867)

Born in Sumner County, Tennessee; died in Lebanon, Tennessee; buried in Lebanon. Served in the Tennessee House of Representatives from 1837 to

1843. Was a veteran of the Mexican War, serving under William Trousdale, whom he followed to the governor's chair. Served as the last Whig governor of Tennessee from 1851 to 1853. A strong Unionist during the War Between the States, he took no active part in the conflict. After the War, he was again elected to the Tennessee House of Representatives, serving from 1866 to his death in 1867.

CANNON, Newton (May 22, 1781—September 16, 1841)

Born in Guilford County, North Carolina; died in Nashville, Tennessee; buried near Triune, Tennessee. Served in the Tennessee Senate from 1811 to 1813 and again from 1829 to 1831. Served in the United States House of Representatives from 1814 to 1817 and from 1819 to 1823. Was the first Whig governor of Tennessee, serving from 1835 to 1839. Formerly called National Republicans, the Whigs were anti-Andrew Jackson and supported Hugh Lawson White of Tennessee as Jackson's successor to the presidency instead of Martin Van Buren. Cannon County, Tennessee, is named in Cannon's honor.

CARMACK, Edward Ward (November 5, 1858—November 9, 1908)

Born near Castalian Springs, Tennessee; died in Nashville, Tennessee; buried in Columbia, Tennessee. Practiced law in Columbia, Tennessee. Served in the Tennessee House of Representatives from 1885 to 1887. Became the editor of the Memphis *Commercial Appeal* in 1892. Served in the United States House of Representatives from 1897 to 1901. Served in the United States Senate from 1901 to 1907. Was assassinated by political enemies on Seventh Avenue, North, in Nashville.

CARR, John (September 5, 1773—1857)

Born near Ramshouses Mill, South Carolina; died near Gallatin, Tennessee. Was an early Tennessee pioneer, living in Sumner County where he helped build forts and stations to protect the settlers from Indians. Wrote a very important book, entitled *Early Times in Middle Tennessee*, which surveyed the trials and tribulations of the Cumberland Valley's early settlement.

CARRICK, Samuel (July 17, 1760—August 17, 1809)

Born in York County, Pennsylvania; died in Knoxville, Tennessee (?). Was licensed as a Presbyterian minister in 1782. Was a traveling missionary in Tennessee. Was pastor of the first church in Knoxville, Tennessee from 1791 to 1809. Was president of Blount College, later to become the University of Tennessee, from 1794 to 1809.

CARRINGTON, Frances Courtney (January 14, 1845—1911)

Born in Franklin, Tennessee; died in Hyde Park, Massachusetts. Was a Union nurse during the War Between the States. Was honored at the Chicago Sanitary Fair. Was a prolific writer, among her works being *The Flag in Dixie, Army Life in the Plains,* and *History of the Indian War of 1866-67.*

CARROLL, William (March 3, 1788—March 22, 1844)

Born near Pittsburg, Pennsylvania; died in Nashville, Tennessee. Moved to Nashville to become a merchant. Was a close friend of Andrew Jackson. Was a colonel in the Creek War of 1813, becoming a major general in 1814. Was governor of Tennessee from 1821 to 1827 and from 1829 to 1835. His administration was known for its reform policies.

Colyar: *Life and Times of Andrew Jackson*

CARROLL, William Henry (February 18, 1843—1916)

Born in Panola County, Mississippi; died in Memphis, Tennessee. Attended the University of Tennessee. Enlisted in the Confederate Army in 1861. Was adjutant of the Thirty-seventh Tennessee Regiment. After the war was engaged in the cotton business in Memphis. Was admitted to the bar in 1875.

Was a leading figure in Tennessee Democratic politics.

CARTER, Landon (January 29, 1760—June 5, 1800)

Born in Virginia; died in Tennessee. Was a Revolutionary War veteran. Was the secretary of state for the State of Franklin from 1784 to 1789. Was the speaker of the senate for the State of Franklin. Was an incorporator of Martin Academy. Carter County, Tennessee, is named in his honor, and Elizabethton, Tennessee, is named for his wife.

CARTER, Samuel Powatan (August 6, 1819—May 26, 1891)

Born in Elizabethton, Tennessee; died in Washington, D.C.; buried in Washington, D.C. Was graduated from the United States Naval Academy in 1846. Became a Union Army brigadier general in the Tennessee volunteers in 1862. Was commissioned a lieutenant commander in the United States Navy in 1863 and a captain in 1870. Was the commandant of the United States Naval Academy from 1870 to 1873. Was promoted to rear admiral in 1882. Carter was the only person in American history to be both an admiral in the Navy and a general in the Army.

CARTER, William Blount (October 22, 1792—April 17, 1848)

Born in Elizabethton, Tennessee; died in Elizabethton; buried in Elizabethton. Was a veteran of the War of 1812. Served in the Tennessee Senate from 1823 to 1825. Served in the Tennessee House of Representatives from 1829 to 1831. Served in the United States House of Representatives as a Whig from 1835 to 1841. Was the son of Landon Carter.

CARTWRIGHT, Peter (September 1, 1785—September 25, 1872)

Born in Amherst County, Virginia; died in Pleasant Plains, Illinois. Was ordained a deacon in the Methodist Church in 1806 and an elder in 1808. Was a circuit rider in Tennessee. Ran for the United States Congress against Abraham Lincoln and lost in 1846.

CARUTHERS, Robert Looney (July 31, 1800—October 2, 1882)

Born in Smith County, Tennessee; died in Lebanon, Tennessee; buried in Lebanon. Was admitted to the Tennessee bar in 1827. Served as the state attorney from 1827 to 1832. Was a member of the Tennessee House of Representatives from 1835 to 1837. Was a founder of Cumberland University and also a founder of its law school in 1847. Served in the United States House of Representatives from 1841 to 1843. Was judge on the Tennessee Supreme Court from 1852 to 1861. Was elected governor of Tennessee in 1863, but because of the state's military occupation, never served.

CATE, Horace Nelson (January 19, 1863—April 11, 1925)

Born in Sevier County, Tennessee; died in Knoxville, Tennessee. Was educated at Carson-Newman College at Jefferson City, Tennessee. Was admitted to the Tennessee bar in 1888. Served in the Tennessee Senate from 1903 to 1905. Was judge of the court of civil appeals from 1911 to 1912.

CATES, Charles Theodore, Jr. (March 6, 1863—October 15, 1938)

Born in Maryville, Tennessee; died in Knoxville, Tennessee. Was graduated from Maryville College in 1881. Was admitted to the Tennessee bar in 1883. Moved to Knoxville in 1889. Became the attorney general of Tennessee in 1902 and served for two terms.

CATRON, John (1786—May 30, 1865)

Born in Grayson County, Virginia; died in Nashville, Tennessee; buried in Nashville. Served with Andrew Jackson in the War of 1812. Practiced law later in Nashville. Was elected judge of the Tennessee Supreme Court of Errors and Appeals in 1824 and served until 1836. In 1837, President Martin Van Buren appointed him associate justice of the United States Supreme Court, a position he held until his death.

Green: Lives of the Judges of the Supreme Court of Tennessee

CHAMBLISS, Alexander Wilds (September 10, 1864—September 30, 1947)

Born in Greenville, South Carolina; died in Tennessee. Was admitted to the Virginia bar in 1884, but began his law practive in Chattanooga, Tennessee, in 1886. Was an insurance executive in Chattanooga. Served in the Tennessee Senate from 1899 to 1900. Was mayor of Chattanooga from 1901 to 1905 and again from 1919 to 1923. Served as an associate justice on the Tennessee Supreme Court from 1923 to 1947, when he was appointed chief justice.

CHASE, Lucien Bonaparte (December 5, 1817—December 4, 1864)

Born in Derby Line, Vermont; died in Derby Line; buried in Brooklyn, New York. Moved to Dover, Tennessee, around 1838. Practiced law in Charlotte. Was elected to the United States House of Representatives from Tennessee in 1845 and served to 1849. Moved to New York City in 1849.

CHEATHAM, Benjamin Franklin (October 20, 1820—September 4, 1886)

Miller: Photographic History of the Civil War

Born in Nashville, Tennessee; died in Nashville; buried in Nashville. Was a captain in the Mexican War. Was a general in the Tennessee Militia upon Tennessee's secession. Was commissioned a major general in the Confederate Army in 1862. Was commander of one of Hood's corps in the Tennessee Campaign during 1864. Saw action at Belmont, Shiloh, Chickamauga, Chattanooga, Franklin, and Nashville. After the war, he served as superintendent of Tennessee prisons for four years. Was appointed postmaster of Nashville by President Cleveland in 1885.

CHEATHAM, Richard (February 20, 1799—September 9, 1845)

Born in Springfield, Tennessee; died near Springfield; buried in Springfield. Was a merchant and stock raiser. Served in the Tennessee House of Representatives from 1825 to 1833 and again from 1843 to 1845. Was a member of the Tennessee Constitutional Convention in 1834. Served in the United States House of Represenatives as a Whig from 1837 to 1839.

CHISUM, John Simpson (August 15, 1824—December 23, 1884)

Born in Hardeman County, Tennessee; died in Eureka Springs, Arkansas.

Moved to Texas in 1837 and became a cattleman. In 1866 he became one of Texas's earliest ranchers to operate in the New Mexico territory. By 1870, he was the largest cattle owner in the United States. Fought in the Lincoln County (New Mexico) range war.

CHIVERS, Thomas Holley(October 18, 1809—December 18, 1858)

Born in Washington, Georgia; died in Decatur, Georgia; buried in Decatur. Was a poet and a good friend of Edgar Allen Poe. Chivers' Tennessee connection lies in the fact that for some unknown reason he had his first book, entitled *Path of Sorrow*, published in Franklin, Tennessee in 1832.

CHURCHWELL, William Montgomery (February 20, 1826—August 18, 1862)

Born near Knoxville, Tennessee; died in Knoxville; buried in Knoxville. Attended Emory and Henry College in Emory, Virginia. Practiced law in Knoxville, Tennessee. Was Knox County Judge. Served in the United States House of Representatives from 1851 to 1855. Was a colonel in the Fourth Tennessee Regiment, CSA.

CLAIBORNE, Thomas (May 17, 1780—January 7, 1856)

Born in Brunswick County, Virginia; died in Nashville, Tennessee; buried in Nashville. Served in the War of 1812 with Andrew Jackson. Practiced law in Nashville. Served in the Tennessee House of Representatives from 1811 to 1815 and was the speaker from 1813 to 1815. Served in the United States House of Representatives from 1817 to 1819. Served again in the Tennessee House of Representatives from 1831 to 1833.

CLAIBORNE, William Charles Cole (1775—November 23, 1817)

Born in Sussex County, Virginia; died in New Orleans, Louisiana. Was judge of the Tennessee Superior Court from 1796 to 1797. Served in the United States House of Representatives, succeeding Andrew Jackson. In 1801, President Thomas Jefferson appointed him governor of the Mississippi Territory. Later, was appointed to the governorship of the Territory of

Taylor: *Historic Sullivan*

Orleans. When Louisiana became a state of the Union, he was elected its first governor in 1812. Claiborne County, Tennessee, is named in his honor.

CLAXTON, Philander Priestley (September 28, 1862—January 1957)

Born in Bedford County, Tennessee; died in Clarksville, Tennessee; buried in Knoxville, Tennessee. Was graduated from the University of Tennessee in 1882 and performed post graduate work at Johns Hopkins. Was superintendent of schools in several towns in North Carolina during the years 1883 to 1893. Was professor of education at the University of Tennessee from 1902 to 1911. Was United States Commissioner of Education from 1911 to 1921. Was president of Austin Peay Normal College from 1930 to 1946. Was author of *Effective English*.

CLAY, Clement C. (December 17, 1789—September 7, 1866)

Born in Halifax County, Virginia; died in Huntsville, Alabama; buried in Huntsville. Was graduated from the University of Tennessee in 1807. Was admitted to the Tennessee bar in 1809. Served in the Creek War. Was a member of the Alabama territorial legislature from 1817 to 1819. Was chief justice of the Tennessee Supreme Court from 1820 to 1823. Served in the United States House of Representatives from Alabama from 1829 to 1835. Was governor of Alabama from 1835 to 1837. Served in the United States Senate from Alabama from 1837 to 1841.

CLAYTON, Henry Helm (March 12, 1861—October 27, 1946)

Born in Murfreesboro, Tennessee; died in Massachusetts. Was educated in Rutherford County, Tennessee. Was assistant at the Harvard Astronomical Observatory from 1885 to 1886. Was local forecast official with the United States Weather Bureau from 1891 to 1893. Was employed in Argentine research work in weather forecasting, beginning in 1910 and was forecast official in Argentina from 1913 to 1922. Was research assistant at Harvard from 1943 to 1944. Was the author of numerous books and papers about meteorology, including *World Weather*.

CLEBURNE, Patrick Ronayne (March 17, 1828—November 30, 1864)

Born in County Cork, Ireland; died at Franklin, Tennessee; buried in Helena, Arkansas. Was a brilliant tactician in the Confederate Army. Was promoted to brigadier general in 1862 and to major general later in the year. Was called the "Stonewall Jackson of the West" for his stand at Missionary

Miller: *Photographic History of the Civil War*

Ridge. Fought at Shiloh, Richmond, Chattanooga, Atlanta, and Franklin. Was killed during the Battle of Franklin.

CLEMENT, Frank Goad (June 2, 1920—November 4, 1969)

Born in Dickson, Tennessee; died in Nashville, Tennessee; buried in Dickson. Was a lawyer, FBI agent, and a soldier before becoming Tennessee's youngest governor in 1953. Served as governor from 1953 to 1959 and from 1963 to 1967. Was an outstanding speaker, with one of his greatest moments occurring at the Democratic National Convention in 1956, where he was mentioned as a possible candidate for national office. Was killed in an automobile accident in Nashville.

CLINE, Patsy

See HENSLEY, Virginia Patterson.

CLINGMAN, Thomas Lanier (July 27, 1812—November 3, 1897)

Born in Huntsville, North Carolina; died in Morgantown, North Carolina; buried in Asheville, North Carolina. Was graduated from the University of North Carolina in 1832. Served in the North Carolina legislature in 1835 and in the state senate in 1840. Was a member of the United States House of Representatives from 1843 to 1845 and from 1847 to 1858. Was a United States senator from 1858 to 1861. Was a brigadier general in the Confederate Army. Tennessee's highest mountain is named Clingman's Dome in his honor.

COCKE, John (1772—February 16, 1854)

Born in Brunswick, Virginia; died in Rutledge, Tennessee; buried in Rutledge. Practiced law in Hawkins County, Tennessee. Was a member of the Tennessee house of representatives from 1796 to 1799 and again from 1807 to 1813. Was the speaker from 1811 to 1813. Served in the Tennessee Senate from 1799 to 1801 and again from 1843 to 1845. Was a Creek War and a War of 1812 veteran. Served in the United States House of Representatives from 1819 to 1827. Was a founder of a school in Knoxville for deaf mutes.

COCKE, William (1748—August 22, 1828)

Born in Amelia County, Virginia; died in Columbus, Mississippi; buried in Columbus. Served in the North Carolina House of Commons and the Senate. Was a leader in the attempt to establish the State of Franklin in what is today east Tennessee. Was brigadier general for the State of Franklin from 1784 to 1788. Was a United States Senator from Tennessee from 1796 to 1797 and from 1799 to 1805. Was a circuit court judge in Tennessee from 1809 to 1812, when he was impeached and removed from office. Served in the Tennessee House of Representatives from 1813 to 1815. Was a founder of the University of Tennessee. Moved to Mississippi and was elected to the Mississippi legislature in 1822. Cocke County, Tennessee, is named in his honor.

COCKE, William Michael (July 16, 1815—February 6, 1896)

Born in Rutledge, Tennessee; died in Nashville, Tennessee; buried in Nashville. Was a graduate of East Tennessee College in Knoxville. Practiced law in Rutledge and in Nashville. Served in the United States House of Representatives from 1845 to 1849.

COCKRILL, Ann Robertson (February 10, 1757—October 15, 1821)

Born near Raleigh, North Carolina; died in Nashville, Tennessee; buried in Nashville. Was James Robertson's younger sister. Moved from North Carolina to Watauga with her brother's party. Later, moved to the site of Nashville aboard John Donelson's flotilla. Became the first teacher in what is today middle Tennessee. The land grant upon which she and her husband settled in Nashville is present-day Centennial Park.

COCKRILL, Mark Robertson (December 2, 1788—June 27, 1872)

Born in Nashville, Tennessee (then North Carolina); died in Nashville; buried in Nashville. The wool from his sheep flock won the first prize at the 1851 World's Fair in London. Was a noted agriculturalist and was

Makers of Millions

45

successful in developing the breed of sheep known as Merino into an outstanding wool-producing variety. Was elected to the Tennessee Agricultural Hall of Fame in 1944.

COGGIN, Barbara (February 27, 1939—January 20, 1981)

Born in Nashville, Tennessee; died in New York, New York. Was a Broadway actress and the star of *Gemini*, Broadway's longest running comedy. Was a veteran of *Fiddler on the Roof, Lovely Ladies, Kind Gentlemen*, and *Poor Murderer*.

COLYAR, Arthur St. Clair (June 23, 1818—December 13, 1907)

Life and Times of Andrew Jackson

Born in Washington County, Tennessee; died in Nashville, Tennessee; buried in Nashville. Was a businessman and lawyer. Attended the 1860 convention which nominated Nashvillian John Bell for the presidency of the United States. Was a member of the Confederate Congress in 1863. Was a leader in the group which freed Nashville from the carpetbagging "Alden ring" in 1867. Was a member of the Tennessee House of Representatives from 1877 to 1879. Colyar wrote *Life and Times of Andrew Jackson* at the age of 80.

CONNOR, William Ott (October 8, 1852—February 5, 1934)

Born in Hamburg, Tennessee; died in Highland Park, Texas. Moved to Texas at an early age. Was a manager of a large Dallas department store from 1877 to 1920. Was a founder and president of the Republic National Bank. Was the first mayor of Highland Park, Texas, and was one of the first members of the Park Board for the city of Dallas, Texas.

CONWAY, Elias Nelson (May 17, 1812—February 28, 1894)

Born in Greene County, Tennessee; died in Little Rock, Arkansas. Was the originator of the donation land laws of Arkansas and of the homestead laws of the United States. Was governor of Arkansas from 1852 to 1860. Was the brother of James Sevier Conway.

CONWAY, James Sevier (December 9, 1798—March 3, 1855)

Born in Greene County, Tennessee; died in Walnut Hills, Arkansas. Was the surveyor general for the Arkansas Territory from 1829 to 1836. Was the first governor of Arkansas, serving from 1836 to 1840. Was the brother of Elias Nelson Conway.

COOK, William Loch (December 6, 1869—March 5, 1942)

Born in Hickman County, Tennessee; died in Charlotte, Tennessee; buried in Charlotte. Practiced law in Charlotte and Nashville. Was judge of the Tennessee Supreme Court from 1923 to 1942.

COOKE, Grace McGowan (September 11, 1863—?)

Born in Grand Rapids, Ohio; died in California. Was married to a Chattanooga native and lived there for some years. Was the first president of the Tennessee Woman's Press Club from 1897 to 1898. Was an author of juvenile books, including *Wild Apple* and *Sunny Bunny Rabbit and His Friends*.

COOKE, James Burch (April 1, 1819—April 18, 1899)

Born in Greenville, South Carolina; died in Chattanooga, Tennessee. Was a colonel in the Confederate Army. Practiced law in Athens, Tennessee; Huntsville, Alabama; and Chattanooga. Served as a judge on the Tennessee Supreme Court from 1884 to 1886.

COOKE, Richard Joseph (January 31, 1853—December 25, 1931)

Born in New York City; died in Athens, Tennessee. Was a graduate of East Tennessee Wesleyan University in 1880. Received his DD degree from the University of Tennessee. Was ordained a Methodist minister in 1876. Was professor of theology at Chattanooga University from 1889 to 1912. Was the vice chancellor there in 1893 and was appointed the acting president in 1897. Was the author of *Religion in Russia Under the Soviets*.

COOKE, William Wilcox (?—July 20, 1816)

Born in Virginia. Was appointed by Governor Willie Blount to the Supreme Court of Errors and Appeals in 1815, but died in 1816 while serving.

COOPER, Dale T. "Stoney" (October 16, 1918—March 22, 1977)

Born in Harman, West Virginia; died in Nashville, Tennessee. Was an accomplished musician at the age of 12. Married his musical partner, Wilma Lee, in 1939. Became a member, with his wife, of the Grand Ole Opry in 1957. Had two hits, *Come Walk With Me* and *There's A Big Wheel*, in the top five country hits of 1959. Was one of the Opry's most popular stars during the 1970s.

COOPER, Henry (August 22, 1827—February 3, 1884)

Born in Columbia, Tennessee; died in Tierra Blanca, Mexico; buried in Mexico. Was graduated from Jackson College in 1847. Practiced law in Shelbyville, Tennessee. Was a member of the Tennessee House of Representatives from 1853 to 1855 and from 1857 to 1859. Was a member of the Tennessee senate from 1869 to 1871. Was a member of the United States Senate from 1871 to 1877. Was killed by bandits while mining in Mexico.

COOPER, Prentice (September 28, 1895—May 18, 1969)

Born in Bedford County, Tennessee; died in Rochester, Minnesota; buried in Shelbyville, Tennessee. Received his college training at Vanderbilt, Princeton, and Harvard Universities. Was governor of Tennessee from 1939 to 1945. After his governorship, he served as United States ambassador to Peru.

COOPER, Washington Bogart (1802—1889)

Born near Jonesboro, Tennessee; died in Nashville. As a youngster, moved to Shelbyville, Tennessee. Studied at Murfreesboro, Tennessee, under Ralph E. W. Earl. Also studied under Thomas Sully at Philadelphia. Was the foremost portrait painter in Tennessee during his time, painting 35 to 40 portraits a year. Was commissioned by the Tennessee Historical Society to paint the portraits of all of the governors of Tennessee. Was a brother to William Brown Cooper, also a painter of note.

COOPER, William Frierson (March 11, 1820—May 7, 1909)

Born in Franklin, Tennessee; died in Brooklyn, New York. Was a graduate of Yale University. Practiced law in Columbia, Tennessee, and in Nashville. Was a judge on the Tennessee Supreme Court from 1878 to 1886. In later life, moved to Brooklyn, New York.

COPAS, Lloyd "Cowboy" (July 15, 1913—March 5, 1963)

Born in Muskogee, Oklahoma; died near Camden, Tennessee. Was brought up on a ranch where he learned to play the guitar at age 16. Performed for 204 radio stations between 1938 and 1950. Began performing on the Grand Ole Opry in 1946 with Pee Wee King's Golden West Cowboys. Among his hits were *Filipino Baby* and *Gone and Left Me Blues*. Was killed in an airplane disaster over Camden, Tennessee.

COX, John Isaac (November 23, 1855—September 5, 1946)

Born in Sullivan County, Tennessee; died in Abingdon, Virginia; buried in Bristol, Tennessee. Served as the county judge and county attorney for Sullivan County, Tennessee, and later as the city attorney for Bristol, Tennessee. Served in both the Tennessee House of Representatives and Senate. Was the speaker of the Tennessee Senate upon Governor James Frazier's resignation, whereupon he became governor himself, serving from 1905 to 1907.

CRABB, Alfred Leland (January 22, 1883—October 2, 1979)

Born in Warren County, Kentucky; died in Lexington, Kentucky; buried in Nashville, Tennessee. Was a student at Peabody College in Nashville, Tennessee, in 1914 during the first summer school ever held on the present campus. Was a World War I veteran. Attended Columbia University, the University of Chicago, and Peabody College. Was dean of Western Kentucky State Teachers' College. Joined the faculty at Peabody College in 1927. Taught history and philosophy of education. Was the author of numerous historical novels with middle Tennesse and the War Between the States as the setting, among them, *Dinner at Belmont, Home to Tennessee*, and *Supper at the Maxwell House*.

CRABB, Henry (1793—1827)

Born in Botetourt County, Virginia; died in Nashville, Tennessee. Was the United States attorney for middle Tennessee. Was a trustee of Cumberland College and of the University of Nashville from 1816 until his death. Was a judge of the Tennessee Supreme Court of Errors and Appeals from 1826 until his death.

CRADDOCK, Charles Egbert

See MURFREE, Mary Noailles.

CRAVATH, Erastus Milo (July 1, 1833—1900)

Born in Homer, New York; died in Nashville, Tennessee. Was graduated from Oberlin College in 1857. Received a DD degree from Iowa College. Was the chaplin for the 101st Regular Ohio Volunteer Infantry from 1864 to 1865. Was associated with Fisk University in Nashville from its inception and was the president of Fisk University from 1875 to 1900.

CRAWFORD, F. Marion (August 2, 1854—April 9, 1909)

The Romantist

Born in Bagni di Lucca, Italy; buried in Sorrento, Italy. Turn-of-the-century Romantic novelist (e.g., *Saracinesca; Via Crucis; In the Palace of the King*), and fantastist (e.g. *Khaled,; Wandering Ghosts; The Witch of Prague*). "The Upper Berth," and "The Screaming Skull" are among his classic horror tales. Though living abroad, Crawford was a popular American lecturer. At the Vendome Theater, February 22, 1898, he lectured 3,000 Nashvillians on the subject of his friend, Pope Leo XIII. On the sixty-sixth anniversary of Crawford's death, April 9, 1975, "The F. Marion Crawford Memorial Society" was founded by John C. Moran, at Saracinesca House, Nashville, Tennessee, establishing *The Romantist* (1977-   ) literary journal, and "The Worthies Library" series of books, as well as the "Bibliotheca Crawford-iana."

CROCKETT, David (August 17, 1786—March 6, 1836)

Born in Limestown, Tennessee; died at the Alamo, Texas, buried in Texas. Served in the War of 1812 with Andrew Jackson. Served in the Tennessee legislature from 1821 to 1825. Served in the United States

Jim Farrell: Crutchfield: *Footprints Across the Pages of Tennessee History*

50

House of Representatives from 1827 to 1831 and again from 1833 to 1835. Later, became a political enemy of Andrew Jackson. Was supposedly the author of *A Narrative of the Life of David Crockett*. Was killed during the siege of the Alamo.

CROCKETT, John Wesley (July 10, 1807—November 24, 1852)

Born in Trenton, Tennessee; died in Memphis, Tennessee; buried in Paris, Tennessee. Was the son of David Crockett of Alamo fame. Practiced law in Paris, Tennessee. Served in the United States House of Representatives from 1837 to 1841. Became a merchant in New Orleans in 1843. Was the founder and editor of the *National* in 1848 and of the *Crescent* in 1850. Moved to Memphis, Tennessee, in 1852, shortly before he died.

CROSS, Edward (November 11, 1798—April 6, 1887)

Born in Virginia; died near Washington, Arkansas; buried near Washington. Was admitted to the Tennessee bar in 1822. Was a justice of the Supreme Court for the Arkansas Territory in 1832. Served in the United States House of Representatives from Arkansas from 1839 to 1845. Was president of the Cairo and Fulton Railroad from 1855 to 1862. Became the attorney general of Arkansas in 1874.

CROZIER, John Hervey (February 10, 1812—October 25, 1889)

Born in Knoxville, Tennessee; died in Knoxville; buried in Knoxville. Practiced law in Knoxville. Was a member of the Tennessee House of Representatives from 1837 to 1839 and of the United States House of Representatives from 1845 to 1849. Was a writer and historical researcher. Was one of the organizers of the Knoxville and Charleston Railroad.

CRUMP, Edward Hull (?—October 16, 1954)

Born near Holly Springs, Mississippi; died in Memphis, Tennessee; buried in Memphis. Was originally in the buggy manufacturing business. Was fire and police commissioner in Memphis in 1907. Was elected mayor of Memphis for three terms to 1916 and was elected again in 1939. Served in the United States House of Representatives from 1931 to 1935. Was a very important political "boss" in Tennessee for many years. Was a regent of the Smithsonian Institution.

CRUTCHFIELD, William (November 16, 1824—January 24, 1890)

Born in Greeneville, Tennessee; died in Chattanooga, Tennessee; buried in

Chattanooga. Moved to Alabama, then to Chattanooga, Tennessee, in 1850. Was an honorary captain in the Union Army during the Chickamauga campaign in the War Between the States. Was a leading builder in Tennessee in the years prior to the war. Was responsible for the design of several early buildings on the University of Tennessee campus. Was a member of the United House of Representatives from 1873 to 1875.

CULLOM, Alvan (September 4, 1797—July 20, 1877)

Born in Monticello, Kentucky; died in Livingston, Tennessee; buried in Livingston. Admitted to the Tennessee bar in 1823. Practiced law in Monroe County, Tennessee. Served in the Tennessee House of Representatives from 1835 to 1836. Served in the United States House of Representatives from 1843 to 1847. Was judge of the Fourth Judicial Circuit Court from 1850 to 1852.

CULLOM, William (June 4, 1810—December 6, 1896)

Born near Monticello, Kentucky; died in Clinton, Tennessee; buried in Clinton. Studied law in Lexington, Kentucky, and practiced in Kentucky and Tennessee. Was a member of the Tennessee House of Representatives and the Tennessee Senate. Served in the United States House of Representatives from 1851 to 1855. Was the clerk of the United States House of Representatives during 1856-1857.

CUMING, Alexander (1692—1775)

Born in Aberdeenshire, Scotland; died in London, England; buried at East Barnet, England. Was elected a Fellow of the Royal Society of London in 1720. Singlehandedly coaxed the Cherokee Indians into declaring their loyalty to England in the 1730s. Was offered the Cherokee crown for his friendship with the Indians. Took several Cherokee braves with him back to England. Died a pauper and alone in London.

CUMMINS, James (Ca. 1840—1929)

Born in Excelsior Springs, Missouri; died in Higginsville, Missouri. Cummins came to Nashville, Tennessee, in November or December 1880, with Jesse James (See JAMES, Jesse Woodson). Afraid of the local police and the possibility of being killed by Jesse, who he believed had killed his friend Ed Miller (See MILLER, Edward), Cummins left Nashville in February 1881. Believed to have been involved in various crimes with the James gang, he surfaced after the expiration of the Statute of Limitations, in the late 1890s.

His last years were spent in the Confederate Soldiers' Home in Higginsville, Missouri. He was the last known surviving member of the James gang.

D

DABNEY, Charles Williams (June 19, 1855—June 15, 1945)

Born in Hampden-Sydney, Virginia; died in Cincinnati, Ohio. Was graduated from Hampden-Sydney College in 1873. Attended the University of Virginia from 1874 to 1877. Received his Ph.D. from Gottingen University in 1880. Was professor of chemistry at the University of North Carolina and was state chemist for North Carolina from 1880 to 1881. Was professor of agricultural chemistry and the director of the Tennessee Extension Station from 1887 to 1890. Was president of the University of Tennessee from 1887 to 1904. Was president of the University of Cincinnati from 1904 to 1920. Was the author of *Universal Education in the South.*

DALTON, J. Frank "Happy Jack" (Ca. 1848—August 15, 1951)

Charles Cowden, Courtesy of *The Tennessean*

Buried in Granbury, Texas. Claimed to be one of Quantrill's Civil War guerillas. As carnival worker "Happy Jack" Dalton, he knew Frank James. He helped Kit Dalton of Memphis write his spurious *Under the Black Flag* (1914); aided Frank James imposter Joe Vaughn of Arkansas, and Billy the Kid imposter Brushy Bill Roberts of Texas. Exhibited at the 1948 State Fair, Nashville, Tennessee, as Jesse James; stayed at the Hermitage Hotel and spoke at the Dixie Tabernacle, September 26, 1948. Nashville's James Russell Davis supported Dalton's claim (himself a Cole Younger pretender). Debunked by Carl Breihan and Stella James, Dalton's real identity is an enigma. Dalton also publicized the legend of the "Confederate Underground," or Knights of the Golden Circle, allegedly headquartered for nineteen years on Fatherland Street, Nashville, plotting a second Civil War. (See also JAMES, Jesse; DALTON, "Captain Kit"; DAVIS, "Colonel" James Russell.)

53

DALTON, John W. "Captain Kit" (Ca. 1847—April 3, 1920)

Born in Kentucky; died in Memphis, Tennessee; buried in Memphis. Author of *Under The Black Flag*, a spurious "memoir" dealing with alleged service with Quantrill's guerillas in Kansas and Missouri, published in Memphis. Evidence in the form of death, census and military records indicate otherwise. "Captain Kit" was a private in Company G, Seventh Tennessee Cavalry, from September 25, 1863, until his desertion on March 25, 1864. He reportedly spent the remainder of the war hiding in Calloway County, Kentucky, where his parents lived. Regardless, the "memoir" has been taken by some as genuine. It was probably written with help from J. Frank Dalton. (See DALTON, J. Frank.)

DAUGHERTY, James Alexander (August 30, 1847—?)

Born in Athens, Tennessee; died in Missouri. Moved to Missouri in 1867. Was a farmer and a banker. Was associate judge for the Western District, Jasper County, Missouri. Served in the Missouri House of Representatives and in the United States House of Representatives from Missouri from 1911 to 1913.

DAVIDSON, Donald Grady (August 18, 1893—April 25, 1968)

Born in Campbellsville, Tennessee; died in Nashville, Tennessee; buried in Nashville. Was graduated from Branham and Hughes School in Spring Hill, Tennessee in 1909. Received his A.B. from Vanderbilt University in 1917; A.M. in 1922. Was professor of English at Vanderbilt from 1937 to 1964; professor emeritus from 1964 to 1968. Was author of *An Outland Piper, Lee in the Mountains,* and *The Tennessee River,* among others.

DAVIS, "Colonel" James Russell (October 1, 1840—March 12, 1950)

Born in Columbia, Republic of Texas; buried in Nashville, Tennessee. May have served with Quantrill's Civil War guerillas; mentioned in William Drannan's *Thirty-One years in the Mountains and on the Plains* (1899). Davis tried to enlist in World War II, boasting his prowess with a pistol (he always wore one to bed); he attempted to enter a cross-country car race, renewing his driver's license at the alleged age of

Charles Cowden, Courtesy of *The Tennessean*

108. In 1948, on his Nashville visit, he supported J. Frank Dalton's claim to be Jesse James, appearing with Dalton on "We the People" TV show, January 13, 1950, and at the court hearing, March 10, 1950. Davis also claimed to be the secretly-surviving outlaw, Cole Younger. He is mentioned in several credulous pro-Dalton books. (See DALTON, J. Frank; YOUNGER, Cole.)

DAVIS, Richard Beale (1908—March 30, 1981)

Born in Accomack, Virginia; died in Knoxville, Tennessee. Was the author of *Intellectual Life in the Colonial South, 1585—1764*, the winner of the 1979 National Book Award. Served on the faculty of the University of Tennessee where he was internationally recognized as an authority on early American literature. A two-time Guggenheim Fellowship Recipient, he also served as a Fulbright Professor in Norway in 1953.

DAVIS, SAM (1842—November 27, 1863)

Born in Smyrna, Tennessee; died in Pulaski, Tennessee; buried in Smyrna. Was attending Battle Ground Academy in Nashville, Tennessee, when the War Between the States broke out. Joined the Confederate Army and became a scout. Was captured in 1863 near Pulaski, Tennessee, with Union information. Was tried by the United States Army and found guilty of spying. Refusing to reveal his contact's identity, his last words were "If I had a thousand lives, I would lose them all here before I would betray my friend or the confidence of my informer." Was hanged at Pulaski, Tennessee, by the Union Army.

DEADERICK, James W. (November 12, 1812—October 8, 1890)

Born in Jonesboro, Tennessee; died in Jonesboro; buried in Jonesboro. Was a state senator from Washington County from 1851 to 1852. Was a presidential elector for John Bell and the Constitutional Union party in 1860. Served as judge of the Tennessee Supreme Court from 1870 to 1886; chief judge from 1876 to 1886.

DE BRAHM, John William Gerard (?—1799)

Born in Germany; died near York, Pennsylvania. An officer of engineers in the Bavarian army, De Brahm came to America in 1751 and helped establish a German colony at Bethany, Georgia. In 1756 he was engaged by the Colony of South Carolina to lay out and build Fort Loudoun in the Overhill Cherokee country, near present day Vonore, Tennessee. An eccentric, De Brahm had a personality conflict with his commanding officer and left the fort in an incomplete state around Christmas, 1756. He was later known among the Cherokee as "the warrior who ran away in the night." During the Revolution he erected the works near Charleston, South Carolina, later known as Fort Moultrie.

DE HAVEN, David William (October 26, 1872—June 4, 1943)

Born in Oxford, Mississippi; died in Memphis, Tennessee; buried in Memphis. Practiced law in Memphis, Tennessee. Was judge of the Tennessee Supreme Court from 1935 to 1943.

DEMONBREUN, Timothy (March 23, 1747—October 30, 1826)

Born in Boucherville, Quebec; died in Nashville, Tennessee; buried in Nashville. Was a veteran of the Battle of Quebec in 1759 in which the British decisively defeated the French. Migrated to the area which later became Nashville, Tennessee, circa 1760. Took up residence in a cave above the Cumberland River and lived there for some years. Moved inside Fort Nashborough after 1780, when the first settlers arrived. Demonbreun Street, in downtown Nashville, is named in his honor.

DE RUDIO, Charles Camilus (August 26, 1832—November 1, 1910)

Born in Belluno, Italy; died in Los Angeles, California. An Italian count, De Rudio was active in the "Young Italy" movement and was involved in an assasination attempt on January 12, 1858, against the life of Napoleon III of France. De Rudio served as second lieutenant of H Troop, Seventh United States Cavalry, at Nashville, Tennessee, from June 1, 1871, to March 10, 1873. He led several detachments to assist internal revenue officers against illegal distilleries in Tennessee. At the Battle of the Little Big Horn, June 25-27, 1876, he narrowly escaped death. He was promoted to the rank of major in 1909. (See also BENTEEN, Frederick William and GIBSON, Francis Marion.)

DESHA, Robert (January 14, 1791—February 6, 1849)

Born in Sumner County, Tennessee; died in Mobile, Alabama; buried in Mobile. Was a merchant in Gallatin, Tennessee. Was a veteran of the War of 1812. Served in the United States House of Representatives from 1827 to 1831. Was later a merchant in Mobile, Alabama, until his death.

DE SOTO, Hernando (1500—May 21, 1542)

Born in Barcelona, Spain; died in Arkansas on the Mississippi River; buried in the Mississippi River. Was governor of Cuba from 1537 to 1542. Landed in Florida in 1539 and is considered to be the first European to set foot in present-day Tennessee. In 1541 he discovered the Mississippi River near the site of Memphis.

DE WITT, John Hibbett (September 21, 1872—March 7, 1937)

Born in Sumner County, Tennessee; died in Nashville, Tennessee. Was graduated from Vanderbilt University in 1894. Received his L.L.B. from George Washington University in 1897. Was admitted to the Tennessee bar in 1897. Served on the Tennessee Court of Appeals. Was a trustee for Vanderbilt University. Was United States fuel administrator for Davidson County, Tennessee, from 1917 to 1918. Was chairman of the Civil Service Commission (Nashville) from 1923 to 1925.

DIBRELL, George Gibbs (April 12, 1822—May 6, 1888)

Born in White County, Tennessee; died in Sparta, Tennessee. Was clerk of the White County Court from 1846 to 1860. Served in the Tennessee legislature from 1860 to 1862. Was a brigadier general during the War Between the States. Served as president of the Southwestern Railroad in 1869. Was a member of the United States House of Representatives from 1875 to 1885.

DICKENSON, David W. (June 10, 1808—April 27, 1845)

Born in Franklin, Tennessee; died in Murfreesboro, Tennessee; buried in Murfreesboro. Was graduated from the University of North Carolina. Was a lawyer. Served in the United States House of Representatives from 1833 to 1835 and from 1843 to 1845.

DICKSON, William (May 5, 1770—February 21, 1816)

Born in Duplin County, North Carolina; died in Nashville, Tennessee; buried in Nashville. Was educated in North Carolina at Grove Academy. Studied medicine and moved to Nashville, Tennessee, where he practiced medicine for many years. Served as speaker of the Tennessee House of Representatives from 1799 to 1803 and served in the United States House of Representatives until 1807. Was a trustee at the University of Nashville from 1806 to 1816. Dickson County, Tennessee, was named in his honor.

DIX, Dorothy

See GILMER, Elizabeth.

DOAK, Samuel (August 1749—December 12, 1830)

Born in Augusta County, Virginia; died in Bethel, Tennessee. Was a graduate of Princeton (then the College of New Jersey). Was a frontier preacher. Founded several churches in Tennessee. Was a member of the convention which formed the State of Franklin. In 1783 he founded the first college west of the Appalachian Mountains, which became Washington College in 1795. Was its president from 1795 to 1818. Organized Tusculum Academy in 1818.

Temple: *East Tennessee and the Civil War*

DONELSON, Andrew Jackson (August 25, 1799—June 26, 1871)

Born in Sumner County, Tennessee; died in Memphis, Tennessee. Was aide de camp to Andrew Jackson in the Seminole War. Was also Jackson's private secretary. His wife served as Jackson's hostess during his presidency. Was charge d'affaires for the Republic of Texas in 1844. Was United States minister to Prussia from 1846 to 1848. and to Germany from 1848 to 1849. Was the unsuccessful candidate for the United States vice-presidency on the Know-Nothing ticket in 1856.

Burke: *Emily Donelson of Tennessee*

DONELSON, John (1718?—1786)

Born in Virginia; died in Kentucky. Was a wealthy landowner in Virginia. Was a surveyor and served in the Virginia House of Burgesses. Assisted in the conclusion of the Treaty of Lochaber between the Cherokees and the British. Moved to Watauga, in what later became Tennessee, in the 1770s, and in 1779 began a river voyage to the site of Nashville. Moved to Kentucky and was later mysteriously murdered on his way to Nashville. His assailant was never caught.

DONNELL, Robert (April, 1784—May 24, 1855)

Born in Guilford County, North Carolina; died in Athens, Alabama. Was a circuit rider in Tennessee and Kentucky around 1805. Was ordained by the Cumberland Presbyterian Church in 1813. Was responsible for popularizing Cumberland Presbyterianism. Was a founder of Cumberland University at Lebanon, Tennessee and was the author of *Thoughts on Various Theological Subjects*.

DORSET, Marion (December 14, 1872—July 14, 1935)

Born in Columbia, Tennessee; died in Washington, D.C. Was the developer of the serum responsible for the prevention of hog cholera. Implemented the meat inspection program at the United States Department of Agriculture, as well as the practice of stamping meat products with harmless ink. Was elected to the Tennessee Agricultural Hall of Fame in 1949.

Makers of Millions

DOUGLAS, Melvyn

See HESSELBERG, Melvyn Edouard.

DRAGGING CANOE (1730—March 1, 1792)

Born in Running Water Town on the Tennessee River; died at Running Water Town. Was the son of the great Cherokee Chief, Attakullakulla. Even though an ally of the British, he fought white expansion vigorously. Consistently led attacks on white settlements in Tennessee. Prophesized that one day his people would "seek refuge in some distant wilderness," a vision which came to pass years later in the Trail of Tears tragedy.

DRIVER, William (March 17, 1803—March 3, 1886)

Born in Salem, Massachusetts; died in Nashville, Tennessee; buried in Nashville. Was a cabin boy at the age of 14; by age 21, he had become a master mariner and was licensed to sail his own ship. Sailed around the world twice and around Australia once. Removed the Pitcairn Islanders, descendants of the *H.M.S. Bounty* crew from Tahiti back to Pitcairn. Later moved to Nashville where he donated his ship's flag, which he called "Old Glory," to the United States Army upon the occupation of Nashville in 1862. For years his grave in Nashville was the only place, other than the grave of Francis Scott Key, where the flag could be flown at night.

DROMGOOLE, Will Allen (1860—September 1, 1934)

Born in Murfreesboro, Tennessee; died in Nashville, Tennessee. Was the literary editor for the *Nashville Daily Banner*. Among her numerous writings were the books, *The Heart of Old Hickory, Fortunes of the Fellow,* and *Harum Scarum Joe.*

DUNLAP, William Claiborne (February 25, 1798—November 16, 1872)

Born in Knoxville, Tennessee; died in Memphis, Tennessee; buried in Paris, Tennessee. Attended Ebenezer Academy and Maryville College. Was admitted to the Tennessee bar and began his law practice in Knoxville in 1819. Moved to Bolivar, Tennessee, in 1828. Served in the United States House of Representatives from 1833 to 1837. Was judge of the Eleventh Circuit Court of Tennessee from 1840 to 1849. Served in the Tennessee senate from 1851 to 1855 and from 1861 to 1863. Served in the Tennessee House of Representatives from 1857 to 1859.

E

EARL, Ralph Eleaser Whiteside (Ca. 1785—September 16, 1838)

Born in England; died in Nashville, Tennessee; buried in Nashville. Came to America as a child. After touring England and France, he returned to America in 1815 and became an itinerant painter in the South. Married a niece of Mrs. Andrew Jackson and became a member of the Jackson household where he specialized in paintings of Andrew Jackson. Died at the Hermitage and is buried there.

EATON, John Henry (June 18, 1790—November 17, 1856)

Born in Halifax County, North Carolina; died in Washington, D.C.; buried in Washington, D.C. Was educated at the University of North Carolina. Moved to Franklin, Tennessee, in 1809. Was a staunch supporter of Andrew

Jackson. Served in the United States Senate from 1818 to 1829. Was United States secretary of war from 1829 to 1831. Resigned his cabinet post over his wife's problems with the wives of other cabinet members. Was governor of the Territory of Florida from 1834 to 1836 and minister to Spain from 1836 to 1840. Was co-author of *The Life of Andrew Jackson*.

Heiskell: *Andrew Jackson*

EATON, Margaret "Peggy" Timberlake (December, 1799—November 9, 1879)

Matthew Brady

Born in Washington, D.C.; died in Washington, D.C., buried in Washington, D.C. Was the second wife of John H. Eaton, Andrew Jackson's secretary of war. Recently widowed, the marriage caused such a furor in Washington that Jackson's cabinet became fragmented in their loyalties, and some authorities believe that vice-president John C. Calhoun resigned his post partially because of this issue. Was a frequent visitor to Nashville and Franklin, Tennessee.

EDMONDSON, William (Ca. 1870—February 7, 1951)

Born in Nashville, Tennessee; died in Nashville; buried in Nashville. Was a primitive sculptor, the son of former slaves. Had little formal education and worked as a servant, fireman, janitor and orderly. Was the first black artist to have a one-man show at the Museum of Modern Art in New York (in 1937). His works were included in the Paris Art Show of 1938 and were widely shown in Nashville, New York, and New Jersey. He is the subject of a book, *Visions in Stone*, by Edmund Fuller.

EDWARDS, John Cummins (June 24, 1804—October 14, 1888)

Born in Frankfort, Kentucky; died in Stockton, California; buried in Stockton. Was educated in Kentucky and began his law practice in Murfreesboro, Tennessee. Moved to Missouri and was secretary of state there from 1830 to 1835. Was member of the United States House of Representatives from Missouri from 1841 to 1843. Was governor of Missouri from 1844 to 1848. Moved to California in 1849 and became mayor of Stockton in 1851.

ELLETT, Henry Thomas (March 8, 1812—October 15, 1887)

Born in Salem, New Jersey; died in Memphis, Tennessee; buried in Memphis. Attended Princeton University and was admitted to the bar in 1833 and practiced law in New Jersey. Moved to Port Gibson, Mississippi, in 1837. Served in the United States House of Representatives from Mississippi in 1847. Served in the Mississippi Senate from 1853 to 1865. Declined an appointment as the postmaster general of the Confederate States of America. Was a judge of the Mississippi Supreme Court from 1865 to 1868. Moved to Memphis in 1868. Was Chancellor of the Twelfth Division of Tennessee in 1886. Died while welcoming President Grover Cleveland to Memphis.

ELLINGTON, Buford (June 27, 1907—April 3, 1972)

Born in Holmes County, Mississippi; died in Florida; buried in Lewisburg, Tennessee. Was a farmer and merchant. Was a close advisor to Governor Frank Clement. When Clement could not succeed himself, Ellington was elected to take over the helm of government. Was governor of Tennessee from 1959 to 1963 and from 1967 to 1971. Amidst the civil rights arguments of the era, Ellington supported integration and appointed a Negro to his cabinet.

ELLIOTT, Lizzie (November 20, 1860—May 13, 1932)

Born in Nashville, Tennessee; died in Nashville; buried in Nashville. Was the daughter of Dr. C. D. Elliott, the president of Nashville Female Academy. Graduated from the University of Nashville in 1881. Taught in public and private schools in Nashville for over 50 years. Was an officer of the Tennessee Historical Society, was instrumental in the rebuilding of Fort Nashborough and was the author of *Early History of Nashville.*

EMBREE, Elihu (November 11, 1782—December 4, 1820)

Born in Pennsylvania; died in Tennessee. Was an early iron manufacturer in Tennessee. He converted to the Society of Friends and freed his slaves in 1815. Established the *Manumission Intelligencer* and later the *Emancipator* at Jonesboro, Tennessee. The *Manumission Intelligencer* was the first journal in the United States completely devoted to the anti-slavery movement.

EMMERSON, Thomas (June 23, 1773—?)

Born in Virginia; died in Jonesboro, Tennessee; buried in Jonesboro. Was the first mayor of Knoxville, Tennessee. Was a founder of Hampden-Sydney Academy. Was a judge of the Tennessee Superior Court from 1807 to 1809 and of its successor, the Supreme Court of Errors and Appeals from 1819 to 1822.

ENLOE, Benjamin Augustine (January 18, 1848—July 9, 1922)

Born in Clarksburg, Tennessee; died in Jackson, Tennessee. Was educated at Bethel University and Cumberland University. Was a member of the Tennessee House of Representatives from 1869 to 1872. Was admitted to the Tennessee bar in 1873. Served as editor of the Jackson (Tennessee) *Tribune and Sun* from 1874 to 1886. Served in the United States House of Representatives from 1887 to 1895. Was executive commissioner for Tennessee at the St. Louis Exposition in 1904 and was chairman of the Tennessee Railroad Commission.

ETHERIDGE, Emerson (September 28, 1819—October 21, 1902)

Born in Currituck County, North Carolina; died in Dresden, Tennessee (?). Moved to Tennessee at a young age; became a lawyer in 1840. Served in the Tennessee House of Representatives in 1845. Served in the United States House of Representatives from 1853 to 1857 and from 1859 to 1861. Was the last Whig member of Congress. Ran for governor of Tennessee in 1867, but was defeated by William G. Brownlow. Served in the state senate in 1869. Was surveyor of customs at Memphis from 1891 to 1894.

EVANS, Henry C. (June 18, 1843—December 12, 1921)

Born in Juniata County, Pennsylvania; died in Chattanooga, Tennessee. Was a member of the Forty-first Wisconsin Infantry during the War Between the States. After the war, he located in Chattanooga where he was involved in iron working and rail car manufacturing. Was twice mayor of Chattanooga. Served in the United States House of Representatives from 1889 to 1891. Popular returns in 1894 indicated Evans had won the governorship of Tennessee, but a recount showed his opponent, Turney, had actually won. Ran second in the race for United States vice-president in 1896. Was commissioner of pensions from 1897 to 1902. Served as American consul to London from 1902 to 1905.

EVE, Paul Fitzsimons (June 27, 1806—November 3, 1877)

Born in Augusta, Georgia; died in Nashville, Tennessee; buried in Nashville. Received his M.D. from the University of Pennsylvania in 1828 and practiced medicine in London and Paris. Served in a hospital in Warsaw. Was an organizer of the Medical College of Georgia in 1832 and was professor of surgery at the University of Nashville from 1851 to 1861 and from 1870 to 1877. Served in the Mexican War and was surgeon general of Tennessee during the War Between the States. Was president of the American Medical Association from 1857 to 1858. Was the first American surgeon to perform a hysterectomy. Was the author of several medical books.

EWELL, Richard Stoddert (February 8, 1817—January 25, 1872)

Born in Georgetown, Washington, D.C.; died in Spring Hill, Tennessee. Served in the Mexican War and the Indian Wars of 1857-59. Served under General "Stonewall" Jackson in the Virginia valley campaigns. Was promoted to lieutenant general in 1863. Commanded the defense of Richmond. Was considered one of the great Confederate generals. Retired to Spring Hill, Tennessee, where he engaged in agriculture.

Miller: *Photographic History of the Civil War*

EWING, Andrew (June 17, 1813—June 16, 1864)

Born in Nashville, Tennessee; died in Atlanta, Georgia; buried in Nashville. Was graduated from the University of Nashville in 1832. Was admitted to the Tennessee bar in 1835. Was a trustee of the University of Nashville from 1833 to 1864. Served in the United States House of Representatives from 1849 to 1851. Was judge in General Braxton Bragg's military court during the War Between the States.

FANNING, Tolbert (May 10, 1810—May 3, 1874)

Born in Cannon County, Tennessee. Was educated at the University of Nashville. Was a Disciples of Christ preacher. Opened a boarding school for girls at Franklin, Tennessee, in 1837. Opened the first school in the United States to combine agricultural and academic courses in 1843. It became Franklin College in Nashville, Tennessee. Was the publisher of *Naturalist and Journal of Natural History, Agriculture, Education, and Literature.*

FARRAGUT, David Glasgow (July 5, 1801—August 14, 1870)

Harper: *Pictorial History of the Civil War*

Born near Knoxville, Tennessee; died in Portsmouth, New Hampshire; buried in Westchester County, New York. Was commissioned a midshipman in the United States Navy at the age of nine. Grew up in the Navy and spoke French, Italian, Spanish, and Arabic. His attack at Mobile Bay during the War Between the States was his most memorable. The United States Congress created the rank of vice admiral specifically for him in 1864, and then admiral in 1866. Consequently, Farragut was the first admiral in the history of the United States Navy.

FENTRESS, Francis (November 2, 1873—October 30, 1930)

Born in Bolivar, Tennessee; died in Memphis, Tennessee; buried in Memphis. Was judge of the Tennessee Supreme Court during 1918. Was the grandson of James Fentress, for whom Fentress County, Tennessee, was named. Practiced law in Memphis.

FISK, Clinton Bowen (December 8, 1828—July 9, 1890)

Born in New York; died in New York City. Was a major general in the United States Army during the War Between the States. Was assistant commissioner of the Bureau of Refugees, Freedmen, and Abandoned Lands for Kentucky and Tennessee. Was the founder of Fisk University in Nashville, Tennessee, in

1866. Was the Prohibitionist candidate for United States president in 1888.

FITZGERALD, Oscar Penn (August 24, 1829—1911)

Born in North Carolina; died in Nashville, Tennessee. Educated at the University of the South at Sewanee, Tennessee. Entered the Methodist ministry in Georgia in 1853. Moved to California in 1855 where he was superintendent of public instruction for California from 1867 to 1871. Became editor of the *Christian Advocate* in Nashville, Tennessee in 1878. Became a bishop in 1890. Was author of *California Sketches* and other books.

FITZGERALD, William (August 6, 1799—March 1864)

Born in Port Tobacco, Maryland; died in Paris, Tennessee; buried in Paris. Was admitted to the Tennessee bar at Dover in 1821. Was clerk of the Stewart County Circuit Court from 1822 to 1825. Served in the Tennessee House of Representatives from 1825 to 1827 and in the United States House of Representatives from 1831 to 1833. Moved to Paris, Tennessee, and served as judge of the Ninth Judicial Circuit from 1841 to 1861.

FITZPATRICK, Morgan C. (?—June 29, 1908)

Died in Gallatin, Tennessee. Was educated at the University of Ohio, then received his L.L.B. from Cumberland University at Lebanon, Tennessee. Was admitted to the Tennessee bar in 1890. Served as editor of the *Hartsville Vidette* from 1895 to 1896. Served in the Tennessee House of Representatives from 1894 to 1898 and was speaker from 1897 to 1898. Was state superintendent of schools from 1899 to 1903. Was member of the Fifty-eighth Congress from the Fourth District.

FLATT, Lester Raymond (June 19, 1914—May 1979)

Born in Overton County, Tennessee; died in Nashville, Tennessee. With Earl Scruggs, he pioneered a unique bluegrass style of music under Bill Monroe's leadership. In 1939 was heard on Station WDBJ, Roanoke, Virginia. Joined Bill Monroe on the Grand Ole Opry in the 1940s. Left Monroe in 1948 and made his first record with Scruggs. In 1949 recorded *Foggy*

Les Leverett

Mountain Breakdown. In 1953 he began his Martha White Biscuit Show on WSM radio, Nashville. Joined the Grand Ole Opry in 1955. His *Ballad of Jed Clampett* was number one on the country music charts for three months in 1962.

FLETCHER, John Madison (June 27, 1873—December 12, 1944)

Born in Rutherford County, Tennessee; died in New Orleans, Louisiana. Was graduated from Vanderbilt University in 1901 and received his Ph.D. from Clark University in 1912. Became professor and head of the psychology department at Tulane University in 1913; was dean of the graduate department from 1920 to 1924. Was professor of psychology at Vanderbilt University from 1926 to 1928. Authored *The Problem of Stuttering*.

FOLEY, Clyde Julian "Red" (June 17, 1910—September 19, 1968)

Born in Bluelick, Kentucky, died in Fort Wayne, Indiana. In 1939 he appeared on *Avalon Time* with Red Skelton. Was the first country star with a network radio show. His hits included *Tennessee Saturday Night, Candy Kisses,* and *Chattanooga Shoe Shine Boy*. Was a Grand Ole Opry star during the 1940s. In 1954 moved to Missouri and hosted *Ozark Jubilee*, one of the first successful country TV programs.

FOLK, Edgar Estes (September 6, 1856—February 27, 1917)

Born in Haywood County, Tennessee; died in Nashville, Tennessee. Graduated from Wake Forest in 1877; was ordained a Baptist minister in 1882. Was a pastor at Murfreesboro, Tennessee from 1882 to 1885 and edited the *Baptist Reflector* from 1888 to 1889. Was president of the Anti-Saloon League of Tennessee from 1899 to 1911 and wrote *Plans of Salvation*.

FOLK, Joseph Wingate (October 28, 1869—May 28, 1923)

Born in Brownsville, Tennessee. Received his L.L.B. from Vanderbilt University in 1890. Was admitted to the bar in 1890; practiced law in Brownsville for four years. Moved to St. Louis, Missouri, and became active in politics. Was governor of Missouri from 1905 to 1909. Was the author of the Missouri Anti-Lobby Law and the Child Labor Law. Was chief counsel for the Interstate Commerce Commission from 1914 to 1918.

FOLKES, William C. (June 8, 1845—May 17, 1890)

Born in Lynchburg, Virginia; died in Memphis, Tennessee (?); buried in

Memphis. Attended the University of Virginia. Served in the Confederate Army during the War Between the States. Was judge of the Tennessee Supreme Court from 1886 to 1890.

FOOTE, Henry Stuart (February 28, 1804—May 20, 1880)

Born in Fauquier County, Virginia; died in Nashville, Tennessee. Was graduated from Washington and Lee University in 1819; was admitted to the Virginia bar in 1823. Moved to Mississippi and served in the legislature in 1839. Was United States senator from Mississippi from 1847 to 1851. Was governor of Mississippi from 1851 to 1854. Served in the Confederate Congress from 1861 to 1865 and wrote *The War of Rebellion* and *Bench and Bar of the South and Southwest.*

FORREST, Nathan Bedford (July 13, 1821—October 29, 1877)

Born in Chapel Hill, Tennessee; died in Memphis, Tennessee; buried in Memphis. Was a farmer before the War Between the States. Was commissioned a lieutenant colonel in the Confederate Army in 1861; brigadier general in 1862; major general in 1863. Fought at Fort Donelson, Chickamauga and other battles. Promoted to lieutenant general in February 1865. His victory at Brice's Crossroads is considered a classic in military strategy. Surrendered the last Confederate command in arms at Gainesville, Alabama, on May 9, 1865. Was briefly involved with the Ku Klux Klan. Became president of an insurance company in Memphis and later, president of a railroad company.

Miller: *Photographic History of the Civil War*

FORT, Cornelia (February 5, 1919—March 21, 1943)

Born in Nashville, Tennessee; died near Abilene, Texas. Was educated in Nashville, Tennessee, and was graduated from Ward-Belmont. Attended Sarah Lawrence College in Bronxville, New York. Was Nashville's first female flying instructor and the second local woman to obtain a flying license. Joined the W.A.S.Ps. and left Nashville in 1941 for Hawaii. While on active duty, she became the first woman pilot to die in the service of her country when her plane crashed in Texas. The Cornelia Fort Air Park in Nashville is named in her honor.

FOSTER, Ephraim Hubbard (September 17, 1794—September 6, 1854)

Born in Bardstown, Kentucky; died in Nashville, Tennessee. Was educated at Cumberland College. Was admitted to the Nashville bar in 1814. Served in the Tennessee House of Representatives from 1829 to 1831 and from 1835 to 1837; was speaker from 1835 to 1837. Was a member of the United States Senate from 1838 to 1839 and from 1843 to 1845.

FOSTER, Wilbur Fisk (April 18, 1834—March 26, 1922)

Born in Enfield, Connecticut; died in Nashville, Tennessee; buried in Nashville. Came from New England to Tennessee as a rodman with a survey party. In 1855 he was selected as assistant engineer in charge of construction for the Edgefield and Kentucky Railroad and designed many railroad sections in Tennessee. Was a Confederate veteran. Became known during his army service for his accurate maps. Was engineer for construction of the first street railway in Nashville, Tennessee. Designed the horsetrack and grandstands at the state fair grounds (now Centennial Park) in Nashville. Was the director of works for the Tennessee Centennial Exposition in Nashville in 1897. His firm built the replica of the Parthenon in Nashville.

FOWLER, Joseph Smith (August 31, 1820—1902)

Born in Steubenville, Ohio. Attended schools in Ohio; moved to Kentucky where he taught school and studied law. Moved to Tennessee in 1844. Was professor of mathematics at Franklin College in Nashville, Tennessee, for four years. Was president of Howard Female College in Gallatin, Tennessee, from 1856 to 1861. Was the state comptroller during Governor Andrew Johnson's administration.

FRANK, Morris (1908—November 1980)

Born in Nashville, Tennessee. Was a co-founder of Seeing Eye, Inc., an organization established in 1929 to assist blind persons in obtaining guide dogs. Frank owned the first "seeing-eye" dog in the United States, and his leadership of the Seeing Eye organization led to the placement of over 7,400 guide dogs with qualified blind persons.

FRAZIER, James Beriah (1857—1937)

Born in Bledsoe County, Tennessee; buried in Chattanooga, Tennessee. Practiced law in Chattanooga. Served as governor of Tennessee from 1903 to 1905. His administration was noted for its assistance to education. Frazier resigned the governship in 1905 to assume the United States senate seat vacated by the death of William Bate. Served in the senate continuously from that time until 1921.

FREEMAN, Thomas J. (July 19, 1827—September 16, 1891)

Died in Dallas, Texas. Was a colonel in the Confederate Army. After the war he was recognized as one of west Tennessee's foremost lawyers. Was judge of the Tennessee Supreme Court from 1870 to 1886. Was head of the University of Tennessee Law School for a short time.

FRENCH, Lucy Virginia Smith (March 16, 1825—March 31, 1881)

Born in Maryland; died in McMinnville, Tennessee; buried in McMinnville. Was educated at Washington (Pennsylvania) Female Seminary. Moved to Memphis, Tennessee. Later lived at "Forest Home" in McMinnville, Tennessee, from 1853 to 1881. Was a writer and editor for several newspapers and home magazines. Was the author of *Legends of the South, My Roses,* and *Darlingtonia.*

FULTON, William S. (June 2, 1795—August 15, 1844)

Born in Cecil County, Maryland; died in Little Rock, Arkansas; buried in Little Rock. Was graduated from Baltimore College in 1813. Served in the War of 1812. Moved to Tennessee after the war. Admitted to the Tennessee bar in 1817 and practiced law in Gallatin, Tennessee. Was military secretary to Andrew Jackson in the Florida campaign of 1818. Moved to Alabama in 1820 and in 1829 was appointed secretary of the Arkansas Territory. Was governor of Arkansas from 1835 to 1836. Served in the United States Senate from Arkansas from 1836 to 1844.

G

GAILOR, Frank Hoyt (May 9, 1892—April 8, 1954)

Born in Sewanee, Tennessee; died in Memphis, Tennessee; buried in Memphis. Received his A.B. from the University of the South at Sewanee, Tennessee, in 1912; was a Rhodes Scholar to Oxford University in 1916. Admitted to the Tennessee bar in 1919. Served in the Tennessee House of Representatives in 1921; in the Tennessee Senate in 1923. Was county attorney for Shelby County, Tennessee, from 1936 to 1941. Was judge of the Tennessee Supreme Court from 1943 to 1954.

Green: Lives of the Judges of the Supreme Court of Tennessee

GAILOR, Thomas Frank (September 17, 1856—October 3, 1935)

Born in Jackson, Mississippi; died in Memphis, Tennessee. Was graduated from Racine College in 1876. Attended the University of the South at Sewanee, Tennessee and received his D.D. in 1894. Preached at Pulaski, Tennessee, from 1879 to 1882. Was vice-chancellor of the University of the South from 1890 to 1893. Became bishop of the Episcopal Church in 1898. Became chancellor and president of the Board of Trust at the University of the South in 1908. Was the author of *The Christian Church and Education*. Was the father of Frank Hoyt Gailor.

GAINES, Edmund Pendleton (May 20, 1777—January 6, 1849)

Born in Culpeper County, Virginia; died in New Orleans, Louisiana. Was a lieutenant in the United States Army when he surveyed the Natchez Trace between Nashville and Natchez in 1801-1804. Later, he and Nicholas Perkins arrested Aaron Burr, the former vice president of the United States wanted for treason. Was a veteran of the War of 1812; received a gold medal from Congress. Assisted Andrew Jackson in the Creek and Seminole Wars.

Taylor: Historic Sullivan

GAINES, John W. (August 24, 1861—July 4, 1926)

Born in Davidson County, Tennessee; died in Nashville, Tennessee. Was educated locally and was graduated from the University of Nashville. He received his M.D. from Vanderbilt University in 1882 but never practiced medicine. Instead, he became a lawyer and served in the United States House of Representatives from 1897 to 1909.

GARDNER, Frederick Dozier (November 6, 1869—December 18, 1933)

Born in Hickman, Kentucky; died in St. Louis, Missouri. Was educated in public schools in Tennessee and Kentucky. Moved to St. Louis, Missouri, at age seventeen. Assisted in drafting the charter for the city of St. Louis. Was governor of Missouri from 1917 to 1921.

GARLAND, Augustus Hill (June 11, 1832—January 26, 1899)

Born in Tipton County, Tennessee; died in Washington, D.C.; buried in Little Rock, Arkansas. Was graduated from St. Joseph's College in Bardstown, Kentucky and was admitted to the Arkansas bar in 1850. He practiced law from 1850 to 1861. Was a member of the Confederate Congress from 1861 to 1864; of the Confederate Senate from 1864 to 1865. Elected to the United States Senate from Arkansas in 1867 but not seated. Was governor of Arkansas from 1874 to 1877. Served in the United States Senate from 1877 to 1885. Was United States attorney general from 1885 to 1889.

GARLAND, Landon Cabell (May 21, 1810—February 12, 1895)

Born in Nelson County, Virginia; died in Nashville, Tennessee. Was graduated from Hampden-Sydney College in 1829. Was professor of science at Washington and Lee University from 1829 to 1832. Was president of Randolph-Macon College from 1836 to 1846. Was president of the University of Alabama from 1855 to 1865. Was the first chancellor of Vanderbilt University in Nashville, Tennessee, from 1875 to 1893. Was the author of *Trigonometry, Plane and Spherical.*

GARRETT, William Robertson (April 12, 1839—1904)

Born in Williamsburg, Virginia; died in Nashville, Tennessee. Was graduated from William and Mary in Williamsburg, Virginia, in 1858. Was a Confederate Army veteran; fought with General Forrest. Taught at William and Mary from 1866 to 1867. Moved to Pulaski, Tennessee in 1868. Was president of Giles College (Tennessee) from 1868 to 1873. Was associate principal of Montgomery Bell Academy in Nashville, Tennessee from 1875 to 1891. Was dean of Peabody College in Nashville from 1899 to 1904. Was the co-author of *Garrett's and Goodpasture's History of Tennessee*, among others.

GATTINGER, Augustin (February 3, 1825—July 18, 1903)

Born in Munich, Germany; died in Nashville, Tennessee; buried in Nashville. Moved to Tennessee as a young man, living first in Kingsport, then in Bradley and Polk Counties. Practiced medicine. Was pro-union during the War Between the States. Moved to Nashville during the war and was appointed state librarian. Was the author of *Tennessee Flora*, recognized as a classic in its field.

Oakes: *A Brief Sketch of the Life and Works of Augustin Gattinger*

GAUL, Gilbert William (March 31, 1855—December 21, 1919)

Born in Jersey City, New Jersey; died in New Jersey. Studied art under John Brown and L. E. Wilmanth from 1872 to 1876. Won medals from the American Art Association in 1882, the Paris Exposition in 1889, and the Chicago Exposition in 1893, among others. Lived in the Fall Creek Falls area of Middle Tennessee for a while before moving to Nashville, where he maintained an art studio. Noted for his sensitive portrayals of scenes from the War Between the States.

GAYOSO DE LEMOS, Manuel (Ca. 1752—July 18, 1799)

Born in Spain; died in Louisiana. As Spanish governor of the District of Natchez, Gayoso was responsible for the erection of Fort San Fernando de las Barrancas in the spring of 1795. Situated at Chickasaw Bluffs, this was the first white settlement on the present site of Memphis. Gayoso ordered the fort destroyed two years later, in compliance with the Treaty of San Lorenzo, which recognized American claims to present day west Tennessee.

GEERS, Edward F. (January 25, 1851—1924)

Born in Wilson County, Tennessee; died in Wheeling, West Virginia. Was raised around Lebanon, Tennessee, but moved to Columbia, Tennessee, when he was 25 years old. Entered the grand racing circuit in 1879 with the Maury County, Tennessee, trained horse, *Hattie Hunter*. Posted time of 2:16½. His horse, *Hal Pointer*, was the first to break the harness record of 2:10. At Toledo, Ohio, Geers broke a world's record when *Single G* won all three heats in less than two minutes each. Was an internationally known horseman and was killed while racing at the age of 73.

GENTRY, Meredith Poindexter (September 15, 1809—November 2, 1866)

Born in Williamson County, Tennessee; died in Nashville, Tennessee; buried in Nashville. Began the practice of law in Franklin, Tennessee. Served in the Tennessee House of Representatives from 1835 to 1839. Was a member of the United States House of Representatives from 1839 to 1843 and from 1845 to 1853. Was a member of the first Confederate Congress from 1862 to 1864.

GEORGE, David E. (?—January 13, 1903)

Birthplace unknown; mummified and exhibited, not buried; mummy's location today unknown. Elegant, theatrical David E. George committed suicide in Enid, Oklahoma, after confessing to being the fugitive John Wilkes Booth. Finis L. Bates of Memphis identified him as being John St. Helen of Texas, an earlier Booth claimant, and by his body marks as actually being John Wilkes Booth. Bates brought the George/Booth mummy to Memphis, keeping it many years in his garage. Bates's *The Escape and Suicide of John Wilkes Booth* published there in 1907 sold 70,000 copies. After Bates's death the mummy was a widely displayed sideshow attraction, once even stolen and ransomed for money. The story was popularized in *Life, Saturday Evening Post* and recently in *Rolling Stone*. Stanley L. Horn discussed the case in "Was He, or Wasn't He?" read to the Tennessee Historical Society, December 10, 1968. (See BOOTH, John Wilkes; BATES, Finis L.)

GIBSON, Francis Marion (December 14, 1847—1919)

Born in Philadelphia, Pennsylvania; buried in Arlington, Virginia. Gibson was first lieutenant of H Troop, Seventh United States Cavalry at Nashville, Tennessee, in the summer of 1872, taking part in an expedition to Livingston, Alabama, in the fall. Gibson temporarily commanded G Troop at the Battle of the Little Big Horn, June 25-27, 1876, and later took part in the Nez Perce campaign of 1877. (See also BENTEEN, Frederick William; DE RUDIO, Charles Camilus; and WINDOLPH, Charles.)

GIBSON, Henry Richard (January 24, 1836 (37)—May 25, 1938)

Born in Queen Ann County, Maryland; died in Washington, D.C., buried in Knoxville, Tennessee. Was graduated from Hobart College (New York) in 1862. Was a United States Army veteran of the War Between the States. Moved to Knoxville, Tennessee, in 1866 and began the practice of law. Served in the Tennessee Senate from 1871 to 1875 and in the Tennessee House of Representatives from 1875 to 1877. Was the founder and editor of the *Knoxville Republican* in 1879. Served in the United States House of Representatives from 1895 to 1905. Moved to Washington, D.C. in 1912.

GIERS, Carl Cooper (April 28, 1828—May 24, 1877)

Born in Bonn, Germany; died in Davidson County, Tennessee; buried in Nashville, Tennessee. Came to the United States in 1845; to Nashville, Tennessee, in 1852. Was a daguerreotypist, photographic artist, and photographer in Nashville. Served in the Tennessee House of Representatives from 1875 to 1877. Was an originator of the immigration movement in America.

GILLEM, Alvan Cullem (July 20, 1830—December 2, 1875)

Born in Jackson County, Tennessee; died in Nashville, Tennessee. Was graduated from the United States Military Academy in 1851. Served in the Seminole War and on the Texas frontier. Was a captain in the United States Army in 1861. Was adjutant general of Tennessee from 1863 to 1865. Was prominent in the re-organization of Tennessee government after the War Between the States. Was commander of the Fourth Military District (Mississippi and Arkansas) from 1868 to 1869. Participated in the Modoc campaign.

GILMER, Elizabeth Meriwether "Dorothy Dix" (November 18, 1861—December 16, 1951)

Born in Montgomery County, Tennessee; died in New Orleans, Louisiana; buried in New Orleans. Was editor of the woman's department of the *New Orleans Picayune* from 1896 to 1901. Began "Dorothy Dix Talks" column in that paper. Joined the *New York Journal* in 1901. Served with several news syndicates writing advice columns. Author of *Dorothy Dix: Her Book* and *How to Win and Hold a Husband*.

GIRDNER, John Harvey (March 8, 1856—November 25, 1933)

Born in Greene County, Tennessee; died in New York. Was graduated from Tusculum College (Tennessee) in 1876. Received his M.D. from New York University in 1879. Was the first man to graft skin successfully from a dead body to a living one. Was the inventor of the telephonic bullet probe. Was the author of *Newyorkitis*.

GIST, GEORGE

See SEQUOYAH.

GLEAVES, Albert (January 1, 1858—January 6, 1937)

Born in Nashville, Tennessee; died in Pennsylvania (?). Was educated at the United States Naval Academy. Was commissioned an ensign in 1881. Established the navy's first torpedo factory in 1908. By 1915, he had the rank of rear admiral. Received awards from many countries. Was the author of *History of the Cruiser and Transport Force*.

GOLLADAY, Edward Isaac (September 9, 1831—July 11, 1897)

Born in Lebanon, Tennessee; died in Columbia, South Carolina; buried in Lebanon. Was graduated from Cumberland University at Lebanon, Tennessee, in 1848, and received his law degree in 1849. Practiced law in Lebanon. Served in the Tennessee House of Representatives from 1857 to 1859 and from 1887 to 1889. Was a member of the United States House of Representatives from 1871 to 1873.

GOLLADAY, Jacob Sholl (January 19, 1819—May 20, 1887)

Born in Lebanon, Tennessee; died in Russellville, Kentucky; buried in Russellville. Moved to Nashville in 1838; to Kentucky in 1845. Served in the Kentucky House of Representatives from 1851 to 1853; in the Kentucky Senate from 1853 to 1855. Was a member of the United States House of Representatives from 1867 to 1870.

GORDON, George W. (October 5, 1836—1911)

Born in Giles County, Tennessee; died in Memphis, Tennessee. Was graduated from Western Military Institute in 1859. Was a brigadier general in the Confederate Army. Studied law at Lebanon, Tennessee; practiced law at Pulaski, Tennessee, and at Memphis, Tennessee, until 1883. Served with the United States Department of Interior in the Indian Territory for four years. Was superintendent of the Memphis city school system from 1892 to 1907. Served in the United States House of Representatives from 1907 to 1911.

GREEN, Alexander Little Page (January 26, 1806—July 15, 1874)

Born in Sevier County, Tennessee; died in Nashville, Tennessee. Was ordained an elder in the Methodist Church in 1827 and moved to Nashville in 1829. Was active in church reform. Ran a publishing house in Nashville.

GREEN, Grafton (August 26, 1872—January 27, 1947)

Born in Lebanon, Tennessee; died in Nashville, Tennessee; buried in Lebanon. Was educated at Cumberland University in Lebanon, Tennessee. Was a judge on the Tennessee Supreme Court from 1910 to 1947; was chief justice from 1923 to 1947. Was on the bench during the famous

Green: Lives of the Judges of the Supreme Court of Tennessee

Scopes vs. Tennessee "Monkey" trial.

GREEN, Nathan (May 16, 1792—March 30, 1866)

Born in Amelia County, Virginia; died in Lebanon, Tennessee (?). Was judge of the Tennessee Supreme Court of Errors and Appeals and of its successor, the Supreme Court, from 1831 to 1852. Considered by some as one of the greatest jurists in Tennessee history. After retiring from the bench, he became an instructor at Cumberland University at Lebanon, Tennessee.

GREEN, Nathan (February 19, 1827—February 17, 1919)

Born in Winchester, Tennessee; died in Lebanon, Tennessee. Was graduated from Cumberland University at Lebanon, Tennessee, in 1845; received his L.L.B. in 1849. Was professor of law at Cumberland University beginning in 1856. Became chancellor of Cumberland University in 1873. Was the author of *Tall Man of Winton.*

GREEN, William Mercer (May 2, 1798—February 13, 1887)

Born in Wilmington, North Carolina; died in Sewanee, Tennessee. Was graduated from the University of North Carolina in 1818. Was ordained a deacon in Christ Church at Raleigh, North Carolina, in 1820. Was founder of St. Matthews Church in Hillsboro, North Carolina, in 1825; was rector from 1825 to 1837. Served as Protestant Episcopal bishop for the Mississippi Diocese from 1850 to 1883. Was a founder of the University of the South at Sewanee, Tennessee, in 1857; became its chancellor in 1867. Was author of *The Influence of Christianity Upon the Welfare of Nations.*

GROVES, James Robinson (April 10, 1820—June 26, 1893)

Born in Chester, Vermont. Was ordained to the Baptist ministry in 1844. Became the head of the classical and mathematics departments at the University of Nashville in 1844. Became the editor of the *Tennessee Baptist* in 1846. Was the author of *Great Iron Wheel.*

GRUNDY, Felix (September 11, 1777—December 19, 1840)

Born in Berkeley County, Virginia; died in Nashville, Tennessee; buried in Nashville. Was admitted to the Kentucky bar in 1797. Served in the Kentucky House of Representatives from 1799 to 1806. Served as an associate justice on the Kentucky Supreme Court of Errors and Appeals from 1806 to 1807. Moved to Nashville, Tennessee, in 1807. Served in the United States House of Representatives from Tennessee from 1811 to 1815. Served in the Tennessee House of Representatives from 1819 to 1825. Served in the United States Senate from 1829 to 1838 and from 1839 to 1840. Was United States attorney general in President Van Buren's administration in 1838.

Pageant of America

GWIN, William McKendree (October 9, 1805—September 3, 1885)

Born in Sumner County, Tennessee; died in New York City; buried in Oakland, California. Was a United States marshal in Mississippi in 1833. Served in the United States House of Representatives from Mississippi from 1841 to 1843. Served in the United States Senate from California from 1850 to 1861, being one of the state's first two senators. Was instrumental in the establishment of the California mint. Assisted in the survey of the Pacific coast.

Cisco: Historic Sumner County, Tennessee.

H

HALL, Frank Palmer (September 15, 1870—July 10, 1926)

Born in Weakley County, Tennessee; died in Nashville, Tennessee. Was a graduate of Cumberland University Law School at Lebanon, Tennessee. Was a practicing attorney in Dresden, Tennessee. Served in the Tennessee House of Representatives from 1899 to 1901. Was judge of the Tennessee Supreme Court from 1918 to 1926.

Green: Lives of the Judges of the Supreme Court of Tennessee

HALL, William (February 1, 1775—October 7, 1856)

Born in Surry County, North Carolina; died in Sumner County, Tennessee; buried in Sumner County. Lived in Sumner County, Tennessee, practically all of his life. When a child, his family was the victim of numerous Indian raids in the Castalian Springs vicinity. Was speaker of the Tennessee Senate when Sam Houston resigned the governorship in 1829. Hall served as governor until the next election when he was succeeded by his friend, William Carroll.

Tennessee Historical Society

HALLIBURTON, Richard (1900—1939)

Born in Brownsville, Tennessee; died at sea in the Pacific Ocean. Moved to Memphis, Tennessee, as a child. Was educated at Princeton University. In 1921 he began his worldwide travels; he climbed the Matterhorn during the winter, retraced Ulysses' journey, and swam across the Panama Canal. He wrote of his travels in many books. He was killed in a typhoon while aboard a Chinese junk 1200 miles west of the Midway Islands.

HANDY, William Christopher "W. C." (November 16, 1873—March 28, 1958)

Born in Florence, Alabama; died in Memphis, Tennessee (?). Was the son of recently freed slaves. At age 23 he joined a minstrel show. He moved all over the South; was bandmaster at Alabama A&M University from 1900 to 1902 before moving to Memphis, Tennessee, where he played for political candidates and

Jim Farrell; Crutchfield: Footprints Across the Pages of Tennessee History

79

was a band leader. He wrote *Memphis Blues*, originally entitled *Mr. Crump,* during this period. In 1914 he wrote *St. Louis Blues*, one of the outstanding songs of all time, and is known universally as the "Father of the Blues." Was the author of *W. C. Handy's Collection of Negro Spirituals* and two books about other Negro composers.

HARGROVE, Robert Kennon (September 17, 1829—1905)

Born in Pickens County, Alabama; died in Nashville, Tennessee. Was graduated from the University of Alabama in 1825. Was professor of mathematics at the University of Alabama from 1853 to 1857. Became a member of the board of trustees at Vanderbilt University in 1889. Inaugurated the Woman's Parsonage and Home Mission Society of the Methodist Episcopal Church, South.

HARNEY, William Selby (August 22, 1800—May 9, 1889)

Born in Haysboro, Tennessee; died in Orlando, Florida. Was a participant in the Seminole War and a colonel in the Mexican War. Was a ranking cavalry officer in the United States Army in 1847. Defeated the Sioux in 1855. Was in command of the Department of Oregon in 1858 and of the Department of the West in 1861. Retired as a major general in 1863.

HARPE, Micajah "Big Harpe" (Ca. 1768—Ca. 1799)

Died in Kentucky. Was a notorious outlaw who first began operations in East Tennessee, but whose terror spread westward with settlement. He was known as "Big Harpe." His brother and associate in crime, Wiley, was known as "Little Harpe." Micajah was decapitated near Dixon, Kentucky, and his head was hung on a stake at a crossroads which became known as Harpe's Head.

HARPE, Wiley "Little Harpe" (?—February 8, 1804)

Died near Old Greenville, Mississippi. Was an East Tennessee outlaw and brother of Micajah. Called "Little Harpe," he was caught on the Natchez Trace, sentenced to die, and hanged at "Gallows Field" near the Natchez Trace in Mississippi.

HARRIS, George Washington (March 20, 1814—December 11, 1869)

Born in Allegheny City, Pennsylvania; died in Knoxville, Tennessee; buried in Knoxville. Was a steamboat captain in Knoxville in 1835. Became a writer and local humorist. Was postmaster of Knoxville, Tennessee, from 1857 to 1858. Was the author of *The Sut Livingood Yarns.*

HARRIS, Isham G. (February 10, 1818—July 8, 1897)

Born in Tullahoma, Tennessee; died in Washington, D.C.; buried in Memphis, Tennessee. Was admitted to the Tennessee bar in 1841. Served in the Tennessee Senate from 1847 to 1848 and in the United States House of Representatives from 1849 to 1853. Was the secessionist governor of Tennessee from 1857 to 1863. Was aide-de-camp to Generals Albert S. Johnston, G. T. Beauregard, Braxton Bragg, Joseph Johnston, and John B. Hood. Served in the United States Senate from 1877 to 1897; was president pro tem from 1893 to 1895.

HARRIS, Thomas K. (?—March 18, 1816)

Died near McMinnville, Tennessee. Was a practicing lawyer in Sparta and McMinnville, Tennessee. Served in the Tennessee Senate from 1809 to 1811. Served in the United States House of Representatives from 1813 to 1815.

HARRIS, William R. (September 26, 1803—June 19, 1858)

Born in Montgomery County, North Carolina; died near Memphis, Tennessee. Was judge of the Tennessee Supreme Court from 1855 to 1858. Was the brother of Isham G. Harris. Was injured while aboard the steamship *Pennsylvania*, which exploded in the Mississippi River not far from Memphis, Tennessee. He died six days later.

Green: *Lives of the Judges of the Supreme Court of Tennessee*

HARRISON, Horace H. (August 7, 1829—December 20, 1885)

Born in Lebanon, Tennessee; died in Nashville, Tennessee (?). Was a lawyer, United States district attorney for Middle Tennessee, and chancellor of the Nashville division. Served as judge of the Tennessee Supreme Court in 1867 and 1868. Later served as vice chairman of the Republican National Convention.

HASKELL, William T. (July 21, 1818—March 12, 1859)

Born in Murfreesboro, Tennessee; died in Hopkinsville, Kentucky; buried in Jackson, Tennessee. Was educated at the University of Nashville. Served in the Seminole War. Admitted to the Tennessee bar in 1838; practiced law in Jackson, Tennessee. Was a member of the Tennessee House of Representatives from 1840 to 1841. Served in the Mexican War. Was a member of the United States House of Representatives from 1847 to 1849.

HATTON, Robert Hopkins (November 2, 1826—May 31, 1862)

Born in Steubenville, Ohio; died near Richmond, Virginia; buried in Lebanon, Tennessee. Was graduated from Cumberland University at Lebanon, Tennessee in 1847. Attended law school there from 1848 to 1849 and was admitted to the Tennessee bar in 1850. Practiced law in Lebanon. Served in the Tennessee House of Representatives from 1855 to 1857. Was a member of the United States House of Representatives from 1859 to 1861. Became a brigadier general in the Confederate Army in 1862. Was killed in the Battle of Seven Pines.

HAUN, Mildred Eunice (January 6, 1911—December 20, 1966)

Born in Hamblen County, Tennessee; died in Washington, D.C.; buried in Morristown, Tennessee. Moved to Franklin, Tennessee, in 1927; was graduated from Franklin High School in 1931. Attended Vanderbilt University, where she studied under John Crowe Ransom. Received a writing fellowship to the University of Iowa. In 1940 she published *The Hawk's Done Gone*, a collection of mountain tales in natural dialogue. Was book review editor for the *Nashville Tennessean* from 1942 to 1943 and editorial assistant to Allen Tate for the *Sewanee Review* from 1944 to 1946. Became a professional writer for the Arnold Engineering Development Center and in Washington, D.C.

HAWKINS, Alvin (December 2, 1821—April 27, 1905)

Born in Bath County, Kentucky; died in Huntingdon, Tennessee; buried in

Huntingdon. Was a lawyer in Huntingdon, Tennessee. Served in the Tennessee House of Representatives from 1853 to 1855. Was elected to the United States House of Representatives in 1862, but was refused his seat. Was United States consul general to Cuba in 1869. Became governor of Tennessee in 1881, serving until 1883. Also during his career he sat on the Tennessee Supreme Court.

HAWKINS, Harold "Hawkshaw" (December 22, 1921—March 5, 1963)

Born in Huntingdon, West Virginia; died near Camden, Tennessee. Was a guitarist at age 15. Joined the service when Pearl Harbor was bombed; served in the Pacific. Had a hit record, *I Wasted A Nickel*, in 1949. Became a member of the Grand Ole Opry in 1955. His song, *Lonesome 7-7203* was number one on the country charts in 1963. Was killed in an airplane crash two days after his record hit the charts.

HAWKINS, Isaac Roberts (May 16, 1818—August 12, 1880)

Born near Columbia, Tennessee; died in Huntingdon, Tennessee; buried in Huntingdon, Tennessee. Admitted to the Tennessee bar in 1843; practiced law in Huntingdon, Tennessee. Served in the Mexican War. Was judge of the Circuit Court in 1862. Was a member of the Union Army during the War Between the States. Served in the United States House of Representatives from 1866 to 1871.

HAY, George Dewey (November 9, 1895—May 9, 1968)

Born in Attica, Indiana; died in Virginia Beach, Virginia. Was a reporter for the Memphis *Commercial-Appeal*. While on assignment in the Ozark Mountains, he conceived the idea of a country music radio show. Became radio editor at station WMC in Memphis, Tennessee. While associated with Station WLS in Chicago, he originated the National Barn Dance. Moved to station WSM in Nashville, Tennessee, in 1925, where he started a similar barn-dance program. On December 10, 1927, the WSM Barn Dance became the Grand Ole Opry.

HAYS, Harry Thompson (April 14, 1820—August 21, 1876)

Born in Wilson County, Tennessee; died in New Orleans, Louisiana; buried in New Orleans. Was a graduate of St. Mary's College in Baltimore. Served in the Mexican War. Pursued a legal profession in New Orleans. Became a brigadier general in the army of Northern Virginia in 1862; a major general in 1865. Was sheriff of Orleans Parish, Louisiana, in 1866.

HAYS, John Coffee (January 28, 1817—April 28, 1885)

Born in Wilson County, Tennessee; died in California (?). Moved to Texas in 1836. Was a Mexican War veteran. Served as captain in the Texas Rangers from 1840 to 1847. Moved to California in 1849. Was sheriff of San Francisco County from 1850 to 1853 and was appointed surveyor general of California in 1853.

HAYWOOD, John (March 16, 1762—December 22, 1826)

Born in Halifax County, North Carolina; died in Nashville, Tennessee; buried in Nashville. Was solicitor general of North Carolina from 1790 to 1791; attorney general of North Carolina from 1791 to 1793; and judge of the Superior Court of North Carolina from 1793 to 1800. Moved to Tennessee in 1807. Served as judge of the Tennessee Supreme Court from 1818 to 1826. Was a founder and first president of the Tennessee Antiquarian Society (today's Tennessee Historical Society). Was the author of *Civil and Political History of Tennessee* and *Natural and Aboriginal History of Tennessee*, among others.

HEIMAN, Adolpheus (1809—1862)

Born in Potsdam, Prussia; died in Nashville, Tennessee. Was a stone-cutter while preparing for an architectural profession. Moved to Nashville, Tennessee, where he became a noted architect. Was a Mexican War veteran, and during the War Between the States he commanded the construction of Fort Heiman on the Tennessee River. Was captured during the fall of Fort Donelson in 1862. His health diminished and he died from the effects. Some examples of his work are the University of Nashville buildings, the old Davidson County, Tennessee, jail, and the Tennessee Insane Asylum in Nashville.

HENDERSON, Bennett H. (September 5, 1784—?)

Born in Bedford County, Virginia; died in Summitville, Tennessee. Served in the United States House of Representatives from 1815 to 1817.

HENDERSON, Richard (April 20, 1735—January 20, 1785)

Born in Hanover County, Virginia; died in Hillsborough, North Carolina. Moved to North Carolina in 1742. Was a lawyer and an associate justice of the North Carolina Superior Court. Organized the Transylvania Company which purchased millions of acres of western land from the Cherokees. Was the organizer of the plan which resulted in the settlement of Nashville, Tennessee, in 1779-80. Served in the North Carolina legislature in 1781.

HENRY, O.

See PORTER, William Sydney.

HENRY, Robert Selph (October 20, 1889—August ?, 1970)

Born in Clifton, Tennessee; died in Nashville, Tennessee. Was graduated from Vanderbilt University in 1911; did post-graduate work at Queens College in Cambridge, England. Was admitted to the Tennessee bar in 1911 and practiced law in Nashville, Tennessee, from 1915 to 1921. Was assistant to the president of the Nashville, Chattanooga, and St. Louis Railroad from 1921 to 1934. Was the author of *The Story of the Confederacy, Trains,* and *As They Saw Forrest.*

HENSLEY, Virginia Patterson "Patsy Cline" (September 8, 1932—March 5, 1963)

Les Leverett

Born in Winchester, Virginia; died near Camden, Tennessee. Won an amateur dance contest at age 4; learned the piano by age 8. In 1948, she won a trip to Nashville, Tennessee. In 1957, she won the Arthur Godfrey talent contest with her rendition of *Walking After Midnight.* In 1961 her song *I Fall to Pieces* was one of her biggest hits. Became a Grand Ole Opry performer and challenged Kitty Wells as the "Queen" of Country Music. Was killed in a plane crash while returning to Nashville from Kansas City. Was elected to the Country Music Hall of Fame in 1973.

HESSELBERG, Melvyn Edouard "Melvyn Douglas" (April 5, 1901—August 4, 1981)

Born in Macon, Georgia; died in New York City. Was a two-time Academy Award winner for his performance in *Hud* in 1963 and *Being There* in 1979. For several years of his youth, Hesselberg lived on Acklen Avenue in Nashville, Tennessee, while his father was a music teacher at Ward-Belmont College.

HILL, Hugh Lawson White (March 1, 1810—January 18, 1892)

Born near McMinnville, Tennessee; died in Hills Creek, Tennessee; buried near McMinnville. Was graduated from Cumberland College. Was a teacher and a farmer. Served in the Tennessee House of Representatives from 1837 to 1838 and in 1841. Served in the United States House of Representatives from 1847 to 1849. Was a member of the 1870 Tennessee Constitutional Convention.

HOGG, Samuel (April 18, 1783—May 28, 1842)

Born in Halifax, North Carolina; died in Rutherford County, Tennessee; buried in Nashville, Tennessee. Moved to Tennessee from North Carolina. Studied medicine in Gallatin in 1804. Was surgeon of the First Regiment of Tennessee Volunteer Infantry in 1812 and 1813. Served in the Tennessee legislature and then in the United States House of Representatives from 1817 to 1819. Practiced medicine in Lebanon, Tennessee, until 1828, in Nashville from 1828 to 1836, and in Natchez, Mississippi, from 1836 to 1838. Was President of the Tennessee Medical Society in 1840.

HOOD, John Bell (June 1, 1831—August 30, 1879)

Born in Owingsville, Kentucky; died in New Orleans, Louisiana; buried in New Orleans. Was graduated from the United States Military Academy in 1853. Was a cavalry instructor there from 1859 to 1860. Was commissioned a first lieutenant in the Confederate Army in 1861. Was wounded at Gettysburg. Directed the Army of Tennessee, which was defeated at Atlanta and Nashville. Surrendered in May 1865.

Miller: *Photographic History of the Civil War*

HOOPER, Ben Walter (October 13, 1870—1957)

Born in Newport, Tennessee; died at Carson Springs, Tennessee; buried at Newport. Was a veteran of the Spanish-American War. Served as assistant district attorney for the eastern district of Tennessee. Was governor of Tennessee from 1911 to 1915. His administration was one of turbulence and turmoil. Prohibition was an important issue and the deeply religious Hooper was caught in the middle. Hooper remained active in politics until his death.

HORTON, Henry H. (February 17, 1886—July 2, 1934)

Born in Jackson County, Alabama; died in Marshall County, Tennessee; buried in Lewisburg, Tennessee. Was an educator and lawyer by profession. Represented Marshall and Lincoln Counties in the Tennessee Senate. Was speaker of the Senate when Governor Austin Peay died in office in 1927. Served as governor of Tennessee from 1927 to 1933. As governor, he was involved in a conspiracy charge and impeachment proceedings, later dropped, were lodged against him.

HOSS, Elijah Embree (April 14, 1849—April 23, 1919)

Born in Washington County, Tennessee. Was graduated from Emory and Henry College in Virginia. Was ordained in the Methodist Church South in 1870. Preached in Knoxville, Tennessee, from 1870 to 1872, in San Francisco from 1872 to 1874, and in Asheville, North Carolina, in 1875. Was president of Martha Washington College (Virginia) from 1876 to 1881. Was professor of ecclesiastical history at Vanderbilt University from 1885 to 1890. Became bishop in the Methodist Church South in 1902.

HOUK, Leonidas Campbell (June 8, 1836—May 25, 1896)

Born in Boyd's Creek, Tennessee; died in Knoxville, Tennessee; buried in Knoxville. Was admitted to the Tennessee bar in 1859. Served as a colonel in the Union Army from 1862 to 1863. Attended the Tennessee Constitutional Convention in 1865. Served in the Tennessee House of Representatives from 1873 to 1875 and in the United States House of Representatives from 1879 to 1891.

HOUSTON, George Smith (January 17, 1808—December 31, 1879)

Born in Williamson County, Tennessee; died in Athens, Alabama; buried in Athens. Was admitted to the Alabama bar in 1831. Served in the Alabama legislature in 1832. Served in the United States House of Representatives from Alabama from 1841 to 1849 and from 1851 to 1861. Was governor of Alabama from 1874 to 1878. Served in the United States Senate in 1879.

HOUSTON, Samuel (March 2, 1793—July 26, 1863)

Pageant of America

Born near Lexington, Virginia; died in Huntsville, Texas; buried in Huntsville. Was adopted into the Cherokee Indian tribe in 1806. Fought at New Orleans in the War of 1812 with Andrew Jackson. Was admitted to the Tennessee bar in 1818. Was district attorney for Nashville in 1819 and adjutant general of Tennessee in 1820. Served in the United States House of Representatives from 1823 to 1827. Was governor of Tennessee from 1827 to 1829, when he resigned and moved to the Indian Territory. Moved to Texas in 1833; became commander-in-chief of the Texas Army in 1836. Defeated Santa Anna at San Jacinto. Was the first president of the Republic of Texas, serving from 1836 to 1838 and again from 1841 to 1844. Served in the Texas Congress from 1838 to 1840. Was a member of the United States Senate from 1846 to 1859. Became governor of Texas in 1859 and served until 1861 when he was ousted from office for refusing to take the oath to the Confederacy.

HOWELL, Robert Boyte Crawford (March 10, 1801—April 5, 1868)

Born in Wayne County, North Carolina. Attended George Washington University from 1824 to 1826. Was pastor of the First Baptist Church in Nashville, Tennessee, from 1834 to 1850 and from 1857 to 1867. Preached at the Second Baptist Church in Nashville from 1850 to 1857. Was the author of *The Terms of Sacramental Communion*.

HULL, Cordell (October 2, 1871—July 23, 1955)

Born in Pickett County, Tennessee; buried in Washington, D.C. Received his law degree from Cumberland University at Lebanon, Tennessee. Pursued post-graduate work at Notre Dame, George Washington University, and William and Mary. Was admitted to the Tennessee bar in 1891. Served in the Tennessee House of Representatives from 1893 to 1897. Was judge of the Fifth Judicial Circuit of Tennessee from 1903 to 1907. Served in the United States House of Representatives from 1907 to 1921 and from 1923 to 1931, and in the United States Senate from 1931 to 1933. Was appointed United States secretary of state in 1933 and served until 1944, longer than any other man. Was largely responsible for the creation of the United Nations in 1945, and was awarded the Nobel Peace Prize the same year.

HUMES, Thomas William (April 22, 1815—January 16, 1892)

Born in Knoxville, Tennessee. Was graduated from East Tennessee College in 1830. Became the editor of the *Knoxville Register and Watch Tower*. Was ordained a deacon in the Protestant Episcopal Church in 1845. Was president of East Tennessee College from 1865 to 1883. Was the author of *The Loyal Mountaineers of Tennessee*.

HUMPHREYS, Parry Wayne (1777?—1839)

Born in Virginia; died in Hernando, Mississippi; buried in Hernando. Moved to Lexington, Kentucky, then to Tennessee. Practiced law in Nashville and Clarksville. Was judge of the Tennessee Superior Court from 1807 to 1809 and judge of the Supreme Court of Errors and Appeals from 1809 to 1813. Was a member of the United States House of Representatives from 1813 to 1815. Humphreys County, Tennessee, is named in his honor.

HUMPHREYS, West Hughes (August 26, 1806—October 16, 1882)

Born in Montgomery County, Tennessee; died in Nashville, Tennessee. Admitted to the Tennessee bar in 1828; served in the Tennessee House of Representatives from 1835 to 1838. Became attorney general of Tennessee in 1839 and served until 1851. In 1862 he was impeached by the United States Congress for accepting a Confederate judgeship at the same time he was serving as a United States federal judge for Tennessee. Was the author of *Suggestions on the Subject of Bank Charters* and an eleven-volume work on supreme court cases in Tennessee.

HUNTER, William Randolph (October 24, 1843—April 13, 1886)

Born near Nashville, Tennessee. Attended the United States Naval Academy in 1860 and 1861. Served in the United States Navy in 1862. After the War Between the States he entered show business under the name Joseph Bradford. Acted on the stage in the East and wrote articles for newspapers under the name of Jay Bee. Was the author of *Out of Bondage, Our Bachelors*, and other plays.

HUNTSMAN, Adam R. (February 11, 1786—August 23, 1849)

Born in Charlotte County, Virginia; died in Jackson, Tennessee; buried in Jackson. Attended early school in Virginia; moved to Knoxville, Tennessee, around 1807. Was admitted to the Tennessee bar. Began practice of law in Overton County, Tennessee, in 1809. Moved to Madison County, Tennessee, in 1821. Served in the Tennessee Senate from 1815 to 1821 and from 1827 to 1831. Attended the Tennessee Constitutional Convention of 1834. Defeated David Crockett for a seat in the United States House of Representatives and served from 1835 to 1837.

I

INGE, William Marshall (1802—1846)

Born in Granville County, North Carolina; died in Livingston, Alabama; buried in Livingston. Attended schools in North Carolina and Tennessee. Was an early lawyer in Lincoln County, Tennessee. Served in the Tennessee House of Representatives from 1829 to 1833 and in the United States House of Representatives from 1833 to 1835. Moved to Alabama and served in the legislature there in 1840, 1844, and 1845.

INMAN, John Hamilton (October 6, 1844—November 5, 1896)

Born in Landridge, Tennessee; died in New Canaan, Connecticut. Served in the Confederate Army. Later moved to New York and was a founder of the New York Cotton Exchange. Was an organizer and director of the Tennessee Coal, Iron, and Railroad Company. Was an officer in several Southern railroad companies and was a member of the New York Rapid Transit Commission.

ISACKS, Jacob C. (January 1, 1767—1835)

Born in Montgomery County, Pennsylvania; died in Hardeman County, Tennessee. Admitted to the Tennessee bar at Fayetteville, Tennessee, in 1812. Served in the Tennessee Senate from 1813 to 1815. Later practiced law at Winchester, Tennessee. Served as judge of the Third Judicial Circuit of Tennessee from 1818 to 1819. Served in the United States House of Representatives from 1823 to 1833.

J

JACKSON, Andrew (March 15, 1767—June 8, 1845)

Born in the Waxhaw Settlements, South Carolina; died in Nashville, Tennessee; buried in Nashville. Moved to Nashville in 1788; became Prosecuting

Attorney for the Southwest Territory in 1791. Served as Tennessee's first representative from 1796 to 1797. Served in the United States Senate from 1797 to 1798 and again, from 1823 to 1825. Was judge of the Tennessee Superior Court from 1798 to 1804. Defeated the Creek Indians in the Battle of Horseshoe Bend in 1814; became a major general in the United States Army the same year. Was victor against the British at New Orleans in 1815. Was first governor of Florida Territory in 1821. Lost the presidential election in 1824 to John Quincy Adams in a contest that was decided by the House of Representatives. Was elected president of the United States in 1828 and served from 1829 to 1837.

JACKSON, Howell Edmunds (April 8, 1832—August 8, 1895)

Born in Paris, Tennessee; died in Nashville, Tennessee; buried in Nashville. Was graduated from West Tennessee College in 1849 and from Cumberland University in 1856. Served in the Tennessee legislature in 1880 and in the United States Senate from 1881 to 1886. Was Sixth Circuit Court judge from 1886 to 1893. Became an associate justice of the United States Supreme Court in 1893 and served until 1895.

JACKSON, Rachel Donelson (1767—December 22, 1828)

Born in Virginia; died in Nashville, Tennessee; buried in Nashville. Was the daughter of John Donelson, co-founder of Nashville, Tennessee. Accompanied her family on board the flatboat, *Adventure*, from Fort Patrick Henry in East Tennessee to the site of Nashville, arriving in 1780. After an unsuccessful marriage to Lewis Robards she moved back to Nashville from Kentucky in 1790. Married Andrew

Ladies' Hermitage Association

91

Jackson in Natchez, Mississippi, in 1791. After finding out that her divorce from Robards was not legally final, she and Jackson married again in 1794. She died after the election of 1828, and therefore, never became President Jackson's first lady.

JACKSON, William Hicks (October 7, 1836—1903)

Born in Paris, Tennessee; died in Nashville, Tennessee. Was a brigadier general in the Confederate Army during the War Between the States. Afterwards became a stock raiser and owned the Belle Meade stock farm in Nashville, Tennessee. In 1881 his horse, Iroquois, became the first American-bred horse to win the English Derby.

JAMES, Alexander Franklin "Frank" (January 10, 1843—February 18, 1915)

Born near Kearney, Missouri; died in Kearney; buried in Kansas City, Missouri. Frank James and his wife Annie settled in the Bordeaux area of Nashville, Tennessee, in the summer of 1877. Under the alias of Ben J. Woodson, Frank worked as a farmer and in 1880 was employed by the Indiana Lumber Company hauling logs. From 1879 till the fall of 1880, his brother Jesse, alias John Davis Howard, lived with him (see JAMES, Jesse Woodson). A son, Robert Franklin James, was born in Nashville on February 6, 1878. Frank and family left Tennessee on March 26, 1881. Frank returned several times in later years, the last being in 1903 with the James-Younger Wild West Show. (See YOUNGER, Thomas Coleman.)

JAMES, Jesse Edwards (August 31, 1875—March 27, 1951)

Born in Nashville, Tennessee; died in Los Angeles, California; buried in Los Angeles. The son of Jesse James the noted outlaw, and his wife Zee, he was born at 606 Boscobel Street in the Edgefield neighborhood of Nashville, Tennessee. Young Jesse was given the aliases of "Charlie" and "Tim Howard" and did not know his real name until his father was killed in 1882. He was implicated in a train robbery at Leeds, Missouri, on September 23, 1898. Exonerated of charges, he wrote a book in 1899,

Tennessee Western History and Folklore Society

Jesse James, My Father, which includes his early memories of Nashville. He later became an attorney and starred as his father in the silent film, *Jesse James Under the Black Flag*, in 1920. (See JAMES, Jesse Woodson.)

JAMES, Jesse Woodson (September 5, 1847—April 3, 1882)

Born near Kearney, Missouri; died in St. Joseph, Missouri; buried at Kearney, Missouri. Jesse lived briefly in Nashville, Tennessee, during 1875. In 1877 he returned to Tennessee and settled in Humphreys County. Illness and debts forced Jesse back to outlawry in 1879, after moving back to Nashville. Jesse and family lived with brother Frank James (See JAMES, Alexander Franklin) until the fall of 1880. Jesse staged at least two robberies from Nashville: two stage coaches near Mammoth Cave, Kentucky, on September 3, 1880 and a federal payroll at Muscle Shoals,

State Historical Society of Missouri

Alabama, on March 11, 1881. Jesse left Nashville on March 26, 1881, following the capture of gang member Bill Ryan (See RYAN, William). A Jesse James imposter appeared in Nashville in 1948 (See DALTON, J. Frank).

JARNAGIN, Spencer (September 17, 1794—June 25, 1851)

Born in Grainger County, Tennessee; died in Memphis, Tennessee; buried in Memphis. Was graduated from Greeneville College in Greeneville, Tennessee, in 1813; admitted to the Tennessee bar in 1817. Practiced law in Knoxville, Tennessee, until 1837 when he moved to Athens, Tennessee. Served in the Tennessee Senate from 1833 to 1835; and in the United States Senate from 1843 to 1847. Afterwards practiced law in Memphis, Tennessee, until his death.

JOHNSON, Andrew (December 29, 1808—July 31, 1875)

Born in Raleigh, North Carolina; died near Elizabethtown, Tennessee; buried in Greeneville, Tennessee. Moved from North Carolina to Greeneville, Tennessee, in 1826. Worked as a tailor. Was an alderman in Greeneville from 1828 to 1830; was mayor of Greeneville from 1830 to 1834. Served in the

Tennessee Senate from 1835 to 1837 and from 1839 to 1841. Served in the United States House of Representatives from 1843 to 1853. Was governor of Tennessee from 1853 to 1857, then a member of the United States Senate from 1857 to 1862. Appointed military governor of Tennessee in 1862. Was elected United States vice president in 1864 and served during 1865. Became president of the United States in 1865 upon Lincoln's assassination, serving until 1869. Was acquitted of impeachment charges in 1868. Later served in the United States Senate in 1875.

Harper's Pictorial History of the Civil War

JOHNSON, Bushrod Rust (October 7, 1817—September 12, 1880)

Miller: Photographic History of the Civil War

Born in Belmont County, Ohio; died in Brighton, Illinois; buried in Brighton. Was graduated from the United States Military Academy in 1840. Was a Mexican War veteran. Was an instructor at the Western Military Institute in Georgetown, Kentucky. Was a colonel in the Tennessee Militia from 1854 to 1861. Served as superintendent of the Military College at the University of Nashville in 1855. Became a brigadier general in the Confederate Army in 1862; a major general in 1863 and saw action at Shiloh, Stones River, and Chickamauga. Was with General Lee at the Appomatox surrender. Became chancellor of the University of Nashville in 1870.

JOHNSON, Cave (January 11, 1793—November 23, 1866)

Born in Springfield, Tennessee; died in Clarksville, Tennessee. Admitted to the Tennessee bar in 1814. Became prosecuting attorney for Montgomery County, Tennesee, in 1817. Served in the United States House of Representatives from 1829 to 1837 and from 1839 to 1845. Was postmaster general of the United States under President James K. Polk. Was responsible for the introduction of the postage stamp in the United States. Became president of the State Bank of Tennessee in 1854 and served until 1860. Appointed to the United States commission to settle the dispute between the United States and the Paraguay Navigation Company in 1860.

JONES, Francis (?—?)

Died in Winchester, Tennessee. Was a lawyer by profession; practiced in Winchester, Tennessee. Served in the United States House of Representatives from 1817 to 1823. Afterwards, he resumed his law practice in Winchester.

JONES, George Washington (March 15, 1806—November 14, 1884)

Born in King and Queen County, Virginia; died in Fayetteville, Tennessee; buried in Fayetteville. Was a saddler by profession. Served as local justice of the peace from 1832 to 1835. Was a member of the Tennessee House of Representatives from 1835 to 1839; of the United States House of Representatives from 1843 to 1859. Served in the Confederate States House of Representatives from 1862 to 1864. Was a delegate to the 1870 Tennessee Constitutional Convention.

JONES, James Chamberlain (June 7, 1809—October 29, 1859)

Born in Wilson County, Tennessee; died in Memphis, Tennessee; buried in Memphis. Was the first native-born governor of Tennessee, serving from 1841 to 1845. Called "Lean Jimmy" because of his slender build (over six feet tall, 125 pounds), Jones beat the popular and formidable James K. Polk for the governorship in 1841. Also served in the United States Senate and as president of the Memphis and Charleston Railroad.

JONES, Joseph (September 6, 1833—February 17, 1896)

Born in Liberty County, Georgia; died in New Orleans, Louisiana; buried in New Orleans. Was graduated from Princeton University in 1853; received his M.D. from the University of Pennsylvania in 1856. Served as surgeon in the Confederate Army from 1861 to 1865. Was health officer for Nashville, Ten-

95

nessee, from 1867 to 1873. During this time was responsible for much scientific excavation of Indian remains throughout the Middle Tennessee region. Later became professor at the University of Louisiana. Was the author of *Explorations of the Aboriginal Remains of Tennessee.*

JONES, William Palmer (October 17, 1819—September 25, 1897)

Born in Adair County, Kentucky; died in Nashville, Tennessee; buried in Nashville. Received his M.D. from the Medical College of Ohio in 1840; practiced medicine in Kentucky from 1840 to 1849. Moved to Nashville, Tennessee, in 1849. Was a Union sympathizer during the War Between the States. Was superintendent of the Academy Hospital of the United States Army at Nashville. Was head of the Tennessee Hospital for the Insane from 1862 to 1869. Served in the Tennessee Senate in 1873. Was president of the faculty at the Nashville Medical College from 1876 to 1897.

JOYNES, Edward Southey (March 2, 1834—June 18, 1917)

Born in Accomack County, Virginia; died in Columbia, South Carolina. Attended the University of Virginia and William and Mary. Was professor of languages at William and Mary from 1858 to 1866; at Washington and Lee from 1866 to 1875; at Vanderbilt University from 1875 to 1878; and at the University of Tennessee from 1878 to 1882. Was the co-author of *Joynes-Meissner German Grammar* and other books.

JUDSON, Edward Zane Carroll "Ned Buntline" (March 20, 1823—July 16, 1886)

Born in Stamford, New York; died in Stamford; buried in Stamford. In Nashville, Tennessee, Buntline edited and published the *South-Western Literary Journal and Monthly Review* (1845) and *Ned Buntline's Own* (1845-1846). Buntline was accused of adultery with Mary, wife of William Porterfield. William was killed by Buntline in an altercation on March 14, 1846. Buntline, awaiting a hearing, was crippled for life after jumping from the third floor of the City Hotel to escape Porterfield's enraged relatives. He was lynched later that evening but was cut down. Exonerated of murder, he was branded an "unfit citizen" by the press and left Nashville. The "King of the Dime Novelists" later launched the career of "Buffalo Bill" Cody.

KEATING, John McLeod (1830—?)

Born in Ireland. Fought in the Irish revolution of 1848. Afterwards moved to the United States and ran a newspaper in New York. Moved to New Orleans, then to Nashville, Tennessee. Operated a printing plant for the Methodists in Nashville. Was the editor of the *Nashville News* from 1858 to 1859. Was a Confederate Army veteran. Established a newspaper in Memphis, Tennessee, in 1865, then was editor of the Memphis *Appeal* for 21 years. Was the author of *History of the Yellow Fever* and *History of the City of Memphis*.

KEFAUVER, Estes (July 26, 1903—August 10, 1963)

Born in Madisonville, Tennessee; buried in Madisonville. Graduated from the University of Tennessee in 1924; received his LL.B. from Yale in 1927. Admitted to the Tennessee bar in 1926. Was state commissioner of finance in 1939. Served in the United States House of Representatives from 1939 to 1949. Served as United States senator for one term ending in 1967. Was a vice-presidential nominee. Ran the crime committee in the senate. Was the author of *Crime in America*.

KENNEDY, Sara Beaumont (?—March 12, 1921)

Born in Somerville, Tennessee; buried in Memphis, Tennessee. Worked on various Memphis newspapers. Was the author of *Jocelyn Cheshire; The Wooing of Judith; Cicely, A Tale of Georgia;* and other books.

KENNEDY, Walker (January 8, 1857—1909)

Born in Louisville, Kentucky; died in Memphis, Tennessee. Was educated in Louisville schools. Worked for the Louisville *Courier-Journal* from 1878 to 1881; the Memphis *Appeal* in 1881; and the *Nashville American*. Was the author of *In the Dwellings of Silence* and other books.

KEY, David McKendree (January 27, 1824—1900)

Born in Greene County, Tennessee; died in Chattanooga, Tennessee. Was graduated from Hiwassee College in 1850; received his LL.B. from the University of Tennessee. Practiced law in Tennessee. Was a lieutenant colonel in the Confederate Army. Was a member of the 1870 Tennessee Constitutional Convention. Was a United States senator from 1875 to 1877. Was postmaster general of the United States from 1877 to 1880. Was a United States district judge from 1880 to 1895.

KILLEBREW, Joseph Buckner (May 29, 1831—1906)

Born in Montgomery County, Tennessee; died in Nashville, Tennessee. Was a graduate of the University of North Carolina, specializing in law and scientific studies. Was commissioner of agriculture and mines for Tennessee from 1871 to 1881. Was agent for the Peabody Fund in Tennessee from 1871 to 1873. Was editor of the *Rural Sun*. Served as special expert for the tenth United States census. Was the author of *Resources of Tennessee* and *Tobacco Leaf*.

KINCAID, Robert Lee (May 17, 1893—May 21, 1960)

Born in Blairsville, Georgia; died in Harrogate, Tennessee. Was graduated from Lincoln Memorial University in Harrogate, Tennessee, in 1915. Became secretary of that institution in 1916, serving until 1922. Was editor of the Middlesboro, Kentucky, *Daily News* in 1923 and from 1926 to 1937. Was vice-president of Lincoln Memorial University from 1937 to 1947 and president from 1947 to 1958. Was the author of *The Wilderness Road*.

KING, Austin Augustus (September 21, 1802—April 22, 1870)

Born in Sullivan County, Tennessee; died in St. Louis, Missouri; buried in Richmond, Virginia. Was admitted to the Tennessee bar in 1822. Moved to Missouri and was a member of the Missouri legislature from 1834 to 1837. Became governor of Missouri in 1848, serving until 1852. Was a member of the United States House of Representatives from Missouri from 1863 to 1865.

KIRKLAND, James Hampton (September 9, 1859—August 5, 1939)

Born in Spartanburg, South Carolina; died in Nashville, Tennessee. Received his Ph.D. from the University of Leipzig in 1885. Was professor of Latin at Vanderbilt University from 1886 to 1893. Was chancellor of Vanderbilt from 1893 to 1937. Was a trustee of the Carnegie Foundation; was its chairman in

1922 and 1923. Was a founder of the Association of Colleges and Secondary Schools of the Southern States in 1895; was its president from 1911 to 1912.

KRUTCH, Joseph Wood (November 25, 1893—May 22, 1970)

Born in Knoxville, Tennessee; died in Tucson, Arizona. Received his bachelor's degree from the University of Tennessee in 1915; master's from Columbia in 1916; doctorate in 1923. Was an instructor in English at Columbia University from 1917 to 1918. Was associate editor of *The Nation* from 1924 to 1932. Was professor of English at Columbia from 1937 to 1943. Was the author of *Edgar Allen Poe: A Study in Genius* and *Great American Nature Writing*, among other books.

L

LANE, Isaac (March 3, 1834—December 6, 1937)

Born in Jackson, Tennessee; died in Jackson. Was a bishop in the Colored Methodist Episcopal Church in 1873. Was trustee of connectional property of the Colored Methodist Church and of the Colored Methodist Publishing House. Was president of trustees of Lane College in Jackson, Tennessee.

LANE, Tidence (August 31, 1724—January 30, 1806)

Born in Baltimore, Maryland; died in Hamblen County, Tennessee. Moved to North Carolina, then to Tennessee in 1776. Founded the first permanent church in Tennessee. Moved to what is now Hamblen County, Tennessee, in 1780. He founded and preached in several churches in the area and was the moderator of the first Baptist Association meeting held in Tennessee in 1785.

LANSDEN, D. L. (May 16, 1869—August 8, 1924)

Born in White County, Tennessee; buried in Cookeville, Tennessee. Was chancellor of the Fourth Chancery District of Tennessee. Became an associate judge of the Tennessee Supreme Court in 1910. Became chief justice in 1918, and continued serving on the Tennessee Supreme Court until 1923.

LEA, Benjamin J. (January 1, 1833—March 15, 1894)

Born in Caswell County, North Carolina; died in Haywood County, Tennessee. Was graduated from Wake Forest College in 1852. Moved to Tennessee and practiced law in Brownsville. Served in the Tennessee House of Representatives from 1859 to 1861. Was attorney general of Tennessee from 1878 to 1890. Was associate judge of the Tennessee Supreme Court from 1890 to 1893 and chief justice from 1893 to 1894.

LEA, John McCormack (December 25, 1818—September 19, 1903)

Born in Knoxville, Tennessee; died in Monteagle, Tennessee; buried in Nashville, Tennessee. Was graduated from the University of Nashville in 1837 and admitted to the Tennessee bar in 1840. Began practice of law in Nashville, Tennessee. Was United States attorney from 1842 to 1845. Became mayor of Nashville in 1849. Declined appointment to the Tennessee Supreme Court in 1866. Served as a member of the Tennessee House of Representatives from 1875 to 1877. Was president of the Tennessee Historical Society from 1888-1903.

LEA, Luke (January 21, 1783—June 17, 1851)

Born in Surry County, North Carolina; died in Fort Leavenworth, Kansas; buried in Kansas City, Missouri. Attended school in Hawkins County, Tennessee. Was clerk of the Tennessee House of Representatives from 1804 to 1806. Served under Andrew Jackson during the Indian Wars. Served in the United States House of Representatives from 1833 to 1837. Was secretary of state for Tennessee from 1837 to 1839. Declined an appointment as United States commissioner of Indian affairs in 1850 by President Taylor. Was Indian agent at Fort Leavenworth, Kansas, from 1850 to 1851.

LEA, Pryor (August 31, 1794—September 14, 1879)

Born in Knox County, Tennessee; died in Goliad, Texas; buried in Goliad. Was graduated from Greeneville College. Was admitted to the Tennessee bar in 1817; began practice of law in Knoxville, Tennessee. Was a veteran of the Creek War. Was United States attorney for Tennessee in 1824. Served in the United States House of Representatives from 1827 to 1831. Moved to Mississippi in 1836; to Texas in 1846.

LEFTWICH, John William (September 7, 1826—March 6, 1870)

Born in Liberty, Virginia; died in Lynchburg, Virginia; buried in Memphis, Tennessee. Was graduated from Philadelphia Medical College in 1850. Became a merchant in Memphis, Tennessee. Served in the United States House of Representatives from 1866 to 1867, and was mayor of Memphis from 1869 to 1870. Died en route to Washington, D.C. to carry his contested election to the Forty-first Congress.

LEWIS, Barbour (January 5, 1818—July 15, 1893)

Born in Alburg, Vermont; died in Colfax, Washington; buried in Colfax. Was graduated from Illinois College in 1846; received his law degree from Harvard. Taught school in Mobile, Alabama. Was a captain in the Union Army during the War Between the States. Served in the United States House of Representatives from Tennessee from 1873 to 1875. Moved to St. Louis in 1878; later to Washington Territory where he raised stock.

LEWIS, Meriwether (August 18, 1774—October 11, 1809)

U.S. National Park Service

Born in Albemarle County, Virginia; died in Lewis County, Tennessee. Buried in Lewis County. Was secretary to Thomas Jefferson. Was a leader of the Lewis and Clark Expedition to the Pacific Ocean in 1805 and 1806. Afterwards was governor of the Louisiana Territory. Was killed or committed suicide in what is today Lewis County, Tennessee, while on a trip from St. Louis to Washington, D.C. Lewis County is named in his honor.

LEWIS, Walter "Furry" (March 6, 1893—September 14, 1981)

Born in Greenwood, Mississippi; died in Memphis, Tennessee. Was a street cleaner in Memphis, Tennessee, by day and a blues musician by night though he could not read or write music. Played with W. C. Handy and had a role in the movie *W. W. and the Dixie Dance Kings*. Toured the United States and Europe with the Memphis Blues Caravan.

LEWIS, William Berkeley (1784—November 12, 1866)

Born in Loudoun County, Virginia; died in Nashville, Tennessee; buried in

Nashville. Began a plantation near Nashville in 1806. Was quartermaster for Andrew Jackson during the Natchez campaign of 1812 and the Creek campaign of 1813. Was the second auditor of the United States Treasury from 1829 to 1837. Was a member of Andrew Jackson's "Kitchen" cabinet. Was a Union supporter during the War Between the States.

LIDDIL, James Andrew "Dick" (September 15, 1852—July 1901)

Born in Jackson County, Missouri. Liddil came to Tennessee with Jesse James (See JAMES, Jesse Woodson) and Bill Ryan (See RYAN, William) in the summer of 1880. A participant in the Glendale, Missouri, train robbery of October 8, 1879, Liddil was probably an inactive member of the gang while in Tennessee. He left the state with Frank and Jesse James on March 26, 1881. Following his surrender in 1882 and pardon, Liddil worked as a saloon keeper with Bob Ford, the man who shot Jesse James.

Tennessee Western History and Folklore Society

LINDSLEY, John Berrien (October 24, 1822—December 7, 1897)

Born in Princeton, New Jersey; died in Nashville, Tennessee; buried in Nashville. Came to Tennessee with his father, Phillip, and family in 1825. Was graduated from the University of Nashville in 1839; received his M.D. from the University of Pennsylvania in 1843; received his D.D. from Princeton in 1856. Was ordained a Presbyterian minister in 1846. Served on the faculty of the University of Nashville; became chancellor in 1855. Was an organizer of Montgomery Bell Academy in 1867 and the Tennessee College

Windrow: John Berrien Lindsley

of Pharmacy in 1873. Was health officer in Nashville from 1876 to 1880. Was the author of *Military Annals of Tennessee* and other books.

LINDSLEY, Phillip (December 21, 1786—May 25, 1855)

Born in Morristown, New Jersey; died in Nashville, Tennessee; buried in Nashville. Was graduated from Princeton University in 1804; became its acting president in 1822. Moved to Nashville in 1825 to take over the presidency of the University of Nashville, a post he held until 1850. Served as a professor at the New Albany, Indiana, Theological Seminary from 1850 to 1853.

Halsey: *A Sketch of the Life and Educational Labors of Phillip Lindsley, D.D.*

LINK, Samuel Albert (June 10, 1848—?)

Born near Lebanon, Tennessee; died in Nashville, Tennessee. Was graduated from Ewing College, Illinois. Attended the University of Nashville in 1891. Was superintendent of the Tennessee School for the Blind for seven years. Was president of the Tennessee Female College at Franklin, Tennessee. Was the author of *Pioneers of Southern Literature*.

LIPSCOMB, David (January 21, 1831—1918)

Born in Franklin County, Tennessee; died in Nashville, Tennessee. Was graduated from Franklin College near Nashville in 1849. Became a Church of Christ minister in 1856 and was editor of the *Gospel Advocate* from 1866 to 1913. In 1891 he founded the Nashville Bible School for Boys and Girls, which later became David Lipscomb College on land donated by Lipscomb. Was the author of *Civil Government, Salvation from Sin*, and other books.

LITTLE, Tom (September 27, 1898—June 20, 1972)

Born in Williamson County, Tennessee; died in Nashville, Tennessee; buried in Nashville. Was a student at Watkins Institute in Nashville, Tennessee, from 1912 to 1915. Attended Montgomery Bell Academy in Nashville from 1917 to 1918. Studied privately under artist Carey Orr from 1913 to 1916. Was a reporter for the *Nashville Tennessean* from 1916 to 1923; for the *New York Herald Tribune* syndicate from 1923 to 1924; and for the *Nashville Tennessean* from 1924 to 1931. Was city editor for the *Nashville Tennessean* from 1931 to 1937; was political cartoonist for the same paper from 1937 on. Was a Pulitizer Prize winner in 1957 for best political cartoon.

LOFTON, George Augustus (December 25, 1839—December 11, 1914)

Born in Panola County, Mississippi; died in Nashville, Tennessee. Attended Mercer University, Baylor University, and the University of Nashville. Was a Confederate Army veteran. Admitted to the Tennessee bar in 1867; was ordained a Baptist minister in 1868. Preached in Memphis and Nashville. Was the author of *Harp of Life*.

LOGAN, Harvey "Kid Curry" (1865—June 4, 1904)

Born in Tama, Iowa; died in Glenwood Springs, Colorado. A member of Butch Cassidy's gang, Logan was involved in a shoot-out at Knoxville on December 13, 1901. Three Knoxville policemen were badly wounded in the fight, as was Logan, who was captured on the outskirts of Jefferson City, Tennessee, the following day. Tried and convicted in November 1902, Logan vowed to escape. He overpowered a guard and broke out of the Knoxville Jail on June 27, 1903. Logan attempted to join Butch Cassidy and the Sundance Kid in South America. Failing in this, he went to Colorado, where he shot himself to prevent capture. (See also ROGERS, Annie.)

LONG, James (1793—April 8, 1822)

Born in North Carolina; died in Mexico City. Moved to Tennessee. Was a physician in the War of 1812, and then had an unsuccessful career as a doctor in Tennessee. Became a merchant in Natchez, Mississippi, in 1817 and led an expedition in 1819 intended to open Texas to American settlers. Declared independence for Texas in 1819; was driven out by the Spanish. Attacked La Bahia, Mexico, in 1820, but was captured and sent to Mexico City where he was executed.

LUDLOW, Noah Miller (July 3, 1795—January 9, 1886)

Born in New York City; died in St. Louis, Missouri. Was a member of a theatrical company which toured Kentucky and Tennessee. Visited Nashville often. Married a Nashville girl, Mary Squires, and conducted a dramatic club in Nashville in 1818. Was the author of *Dramatic Life As I Found It*.

LURTON, Horace Harmon (February 26, 1844—July 5, 1914)

Born in Campbell County, Kentucky; died in Atlantic City, New Jersey; buried in Clarksville, Tennessee. Was associate judge of the Tennessee Supreme Court from 1886 to 1893; was chief justice in 1893. Was appointed by President Grover Cleveland to the Sixth Circuit Court of Appeals in 1893. In 1910, President Howard Taft appointed him to the United States Supreme Court.

LUTTRELL, John King (June 27, 1831—October 4, 1893)

Born near Knoxville, Tennessee; died in Sitka, Alaska; buried in Fort Jones, California. Attended school in Tennessee; was a teacher and merchant. Moved to California in 1852; was a miner and farmer. Was admitted to the California bar and began law practice in Oakland in 1856. Owned a ranch near Fort Jones, California, in 1858. Served in the California House of Representatives from 1871 to 1872; in the United States House of Representatives from California from 1873 to 1879, and was appointed special agent for Alaska for the United States commission of fisheries in 1893.

M

McALISTER, Hill (July 15, 1875—October 30, 1959)

Born in Nashville, Tennessee; buried in Nashville. Practiced law in Nashville, was an assistant city attorney, and served in the Tennessee Senate before becoming governor of Tennessee from 1933 to 1937. Was a fiscal conservative, and as governor, was noted for his financial genius. Was a strong supporter of TVA, and during his administration, Norris Dam was completed.

McALISTER, William King, Jr. (July 4, 1850—May 23, 1923)

Born in Nashville, Tennessee; died in Nashville; buried in Nashville. Was the father of Hill McAlister. Was a judge of the Tennessee Supreme Court from 1893 to 1910. Afterwards, was a member of the Vanderbilt University law school faculty.

McANALLY, David Rice (February 17, 1810—July 11, 1895)

Born in Grainger County, Tennessee. Was admitted to the Holston Conference of the Methodist Episcopal Church in 1829. Preached in Tennessee, North Carolina, and Virginia. Was president of the East Tennessee Female

Institute from 1843 to 1851. Was the editor of the *St. Louis Christian Advocate* from 1851 to 1895. Was the founder of Central College in Fayette, Missouri, in 1852. Was the author of *History of Methodism in Missouri.*

McCALL, John Etheridge (August 14, 1859—August 8, 1920)

Born in Clarksburg, Tennessee; died in Memphis, Tennessee. Was graduated from the University of Tennessee in 1881; was admitted to the Tennessee bar in 1882. Served in the Tennessee House of Representatives from 1887 to 1890 and in the United States House of Representatives from 1895 to 1897. Was a candidate for the governorship of Tennessee in 1900. Was appointed United States district judge for West Tennessee in 1905.

McCLAIN, Andrew (April 6, 1826—January 21, 1913)

Born in Smith County, Tennessee. Was a judge of the Tennessee Supreme Court from 1869 to 1870. Afterwards, was United States district attorney for Middle Tennessee.

McCLELLAN, Abraham (October 4, 1789—May 3, 1866)

Born in Sullivan County, Tennessee; died in Sullivan County; buried near Bristol, Tennessee. Was a graduate of Washington College. Was a farmer. Served in the Tennessee House of Representatives from 1823 to 1825 and in the Tennessee Senate from 1829 to 1833. Was a member of the 1834 Tennessee Constitutional Convention. Served in the United States House of Representatives from 1837 to 1843.

McCONNELL, Felix Grundy (April 1, 1809—September 10, 1846)

Born in Nashville, Tennessee; died in Washington, D.C.; buried in Washington, D.C. Studied law in Alabama; was a saddler by trade. Moved to Talladega in 1834, and was admitted to the Alabama bar in 1836. Served in the Alabama House of Representatives in 1838, in the Alabama Senate from 1838 to 1843, and in the United States House of Representatives from 1843 to 1846.

McCORD, Jim Nance (March 17, 1879—September 2, 1968)

Born in Bedford County, Tennessee; buried in Lewisburg, Tennessee. Served as mayor of Lewisburg, Tennessee, for 13 terms, before being elected to the United States Congress and then to the governorship of Tennessee. Was governor from 1945 to 1949. His most noteworthy accomplishment as governor was the passage of the state's first sales tax program. Upon his retirement from the governor's chair, he returned to his Marshall County, Tennessee, home where he owned and published the *Marshall County Gazette*.

McCULLOCH, Ben (November 11, 1811—March 7, 1862)

Born in Rutherford County, Tennessee; died near Elkhorn, West Virginia. Was a Mexican War veteran; led McCulloch's Texas Rangers in 1846. Served in government capacities in Texas and Utah. Was a brigadier general in the Confederate Army in command of Arkansas troops and was killed at the Battle of Elkhorn Tavern.

McDEARMON, James Calvin (June 13, 1844—July 19, 1902)

Born in New Canton, Virginia; died in Trenton, Tennessee; buried in Trenton. Attended Andrews College in Trenton, Tennessee, from 1858 to 1861. Was in the Army of Tennessee; saw action at Murfreesboro and Franklin. Admitted to the Tennessee bar in 1867; practiced law in Trenton. Served in the United States House of Representatives from 1893 to 1897.

McFARLAND, Robert (April 15, 1832—October 2, 1884)

Born in Jefferson County, Tennessee; died in Morristown, Tennessee. Served in the Confederate Army and practiced law in Dandridge, Tennessee. Was judge of the Tennessee Supreme Court from 1871 to 1884.

McFERRIN, John Berry (June 15, 1807—May 10, 1887)

Born in Rutherford County, Tennessee. Was a Methodist circuit rider from 1825 to 1827. Was a missionary to the Cherokee Indians in Georgia from 1827 to 1840. Was editor of the *Southwestern Christian Advocate* in Nashville, Tennessee, from 1840 to 1858. Was in charge of Methodist missionary work in the Army of Tennessee from 1861 to 1865. Was the author of *History of Methodism in Tennessee*.

McKELLAR, Kenneth Douglas (January 29, 1869—October 25, 1957)

Born in Richmond, Alabama; died in Memphis, Tennessee. Was graduated from the University of Alabama in 1891; received his LL.B in 1892. Moved to Memphis, Tennessee. Was elected to the United States House of Representatives in 1911. He was reelected two more terms, then served in the United States Senate from 1916 to 1953. Was the author of *Tennessee Senators As Seen By One Of Their Successors*.

McKENDREE, William (July 6, 1757—March 5, 1835)

Born in King William County, Virginia; died in Sumner County, Tennessee; buried in Nashville, Tennessee. Served in the Revolutionary War. Became a Methodist minister in 1788; a deacon in 1790; an elder in 1791. Became the first American-born bishop of the Methodist Episcopal Church in 1808.

McKINNEY, Colin Pierson (May 23, 1873—April 29, 1944)

Born in Lauderdale County, Tennessee; died in Nashville, Tennessee; buried in Ripley, Tennessee. Practiced law in Ripley, Tennessee. Was chancellor of the Ninth Chancery District. Was judge of the Tennessee Supreme Court from 1918 to 1942.

McKINNEY, Robert J. (February 1, 1803—October 9, 1875)

Born in Ireland; died in Knoxville, Tennessee; buried in Knoxville. Was judge of the Tennessee Supreme Court from 1847 to 1860 and was one of the period's outstanding lawyers in East Tennessee. Just prior to the declaration of war in 1861, he was appointed to the position of peace commissioner and traveled to Washington, D.C. in an effort to settle the differences between the North and the South.

McMILLIN, Benton (September 11, 1845—January 8, 1933)

Born in Moore County, Kentucky; died in Nashville, Tennessee; buried in Nashville. Opened his first law office in Celina, Tennessee, in 1871. Served over 20 years in the United States House of Representatives. Was governor of Tennessee from 1899 to 1903. Afterwards, was the United States minister to Peru.

McMINN, Joseph (June 27, 1758—November 17, 1824)

Born in Chester County, Pennsylvania; died in McMinn County, Tennessee; buried near Calhoun, Tennessee. Was governor of Tennessee from 1815 to 1821. His administration was noted for the expansion of West Tennessee and the formation of many new counties between the Tennessee and Mississippi rivers. Afterwards, he became an Indian agent in southeast Tennessee. McMinn County, Tennessee, is named in his honor.

McNAIRY, John (1762—1837)

Born in Lancaster County, Pennsylvania. Was elected in 1788 by the

North Carolina General Assembly to serve as judge of the Superior Court of Law and Equity for Davidson County (Tennessee), then still a part of North Carolina. Later, he became judge of the Mero District, and in 1796, when Tennessee became a state, he became judge of the Superior Court. McNairy County, Tennessee, is named in his honor.

Green: Lives of the Judges of the Supreme Court of Tennessee

McTYEIRE, Holland Nimmons (July 28, 1824—February 15, 1889)

Born in Barnwell County, South Carolina; died in Nashville, Tennessee; buried in Nashville. Admitted on trial to the Virginia Conference of the Methodist Episcopal Church in 1845; was ordained a deacon in 1848; an elder in 1849. Was elected bishop in 1866. Was the founder of Vanderbilt University in Nashville, Tennessee. Was president of Vanderbilt's Board of Trustees from 1873 to 1889. Was the author of *Catechism on Bible History* and other books.

MALEDON, George (1830—May 6, 1911)

Born in Germany; died in Johnson City, Tennessee; buried in Johnson City. Maledon was one of the more colorful residents of the Federal Soldiers' Home at Johnson City, Tennessee. "I never hanged a man who came back to have the job done over," he used to say. From 1875 to 1896 Maledon served as executioner for Judge Isaac Parker, the famous "Hanging Judge" of Fort Smith, Arkansas. Over a twenty-one-year period, Maledon personally sprang the trap on 60 of the 88 men hanged by Judge Parker's sentence. Sometimes he presided over the hanging of as many as six men at a time. In addition, Maledon was credited with killing five escapees.

MANSKER, Kasper (Ca. 1750—Ca. 1821)

Born aboard a ship in the Atlantic Ocean; died in Sumner County, Tennessee; buried in Sumner County. Was an early explorer and hunter in the Cumberland Valley of Tennessee. Later built Mansker's Station in Sumner County, Tennessee. Was a colonel in the militia; took part in the Nickajack Expedition. Andrew Jackson lived with him for a while as did many travelers passing through the Cumberland Valley. Was a signer of the Cumberland Compact in 1780. Mansker's Station served as an inn and wayside stop for many years.

MARABLE, John H. (November 18, 1786—April 11, 1844)

Born near Lawrenceville, Virginia; died in Montgomery County, Tennessee; buried in Montgomery County. Studied and practiced medicine in Philadelphia. Moved to Yellow Creek, Tennessee, and practiced medicine there. Served in the Tennessee Senate from 1817 to 1818; in the United States House of Representatives from 1825 to 1829.

MARKS, Albert S. (October 16, 1836—November 4, 1891)

Born in Daviess County, Kentucky; died in Nashville, Tennessee; buried in Winchester, Tennessee. Lost a foot and leg in the Battle of Murfreesboro in 1862. Refusing to become medically discharged he became Nathan Bedford Forrest's judge advocate. After the war he practiced law in Winchester, Tennessee, where he resided in the famous "castle," One Hundred Oaks. Was governor of Tennessee from 1879 to 1881.

MARLING, John Leake (December 22, 1825—October 16, 1856)

Born in Nashville, Tennessee; died in Nashville. Was admitted to the Tennessee bar in 1850. Served as editor of the *Nashville Daily Gazette* from 1850 to 1851, and of the *Nashville Daily Union* from 1851 to 1853. Was the founder and editor of *Union and American* from 1853 to 1854. Was appointed United States minister to Guatemala in 1854 by Franklin Pierce.

MARR, George Washington Lent (May 25, 1779—September 5, 1856)

Born in Marrs Hill, Virginia; died near New Madrid, Missouri; buried in Troy, Tennessee. Attended the University of North Carolina. Was attorney general for West Tennessee from 1807 to 1809 and attorney general for the Fifth Tennessee District from 1809 to 1813. Was a Creek War veteran. Served in the United States House of Representatives from 1817 to 1819. Moved to Obion County, Tennessee, in 1821. Was a member of the 1834 Tennessee Constitutional Convention.

MARTIN, Barclay (December 17, 1802—November 8, 1890)

Born in the Edgefield District, South Carolina; died in Columbia, Tennessee; buried in Columbia. Studied law in Columbia, Tennessee; admitted to the Tennessee bar. Served in the Tennessee House of Representatives from 1839 to 1840, from 1847 to 1849, and from 1851 to 1853. Served in the Tennessee Senate from 1841 to 1843. Served in the United States House of Representatives from 1845 to 1847. Was a trustee of the Athenaeum in Columbia, Tennessee, from 1852 to 1890.

MARTIN, Burton McMahan (October 25, 1866—?)

Born in McMinn County, Tennessee; died in Chattanooga, Tennessee. Was educated at the Hayeville Male and Female College in North Carolina and Grant University. Became a deacon in the Methodist Episcopal Church in 1896; became an elder in 1898. Preached in Pikeville, Rockwood, Athens, Maryville, and Knoxville—all in Tennessee. Was director of the Chattanooga Goodwill Industries, Inc. and was a trustee of the University of Chattanooga.

MASON, Samuel (1750—July 1803)

Born in Virginia. Was a captain of the Ohio County, Virginia, militia during the Revolutionary War. Became an outlaw; operated in East Tennessee and later, Kentucky. Frequented Cave-in-Rock on the Ohio River, a hideout for outlaws. Was killed by his own hoodlum friends who attempted to collect the reward for his capture.

MAURY, Matthew Fontaine (January 14, 1806—February 1, 1873)

Lewis: *Matthew Fontaine Maury*

Born in Fredericksburg, Virginia; died in Lexington, Virginia; buried in Richmond, Virginia. Moved to Franklin, Tennessee, at a young age and spent his childhood there. Became a midshipman in the United States Navy in 1825 and wrote of naval affairs for newspapers and periodicals. Was superintendent of the department of charts and instruments of the United States Navy from 1842 to 1855 and from 1858 to 1861. Was a commander in the Confederate Navy from 1861 to 1865. Was professor of meteorology at Virginia Military Institute in 1868. Was the first American to scientifically chart the oceans. Was called the "Pathfinder of the Seas." Was the author of *The Physical Geography of the Sea* and other books.

MAYNARD, Horace (August 30, 1814—May 3, 1882)

Born in Westboro, Massachusetts; died in Knoxville, Tennessee. Was graduated from Amherst College in 1838. Taught at the University of East Tennessee from 1839 to 1841. Admitted to the Tennessee bar in 1844; practiced law in Knoxville. Served in the United States House of Representatives from 1857 to 1863 and from 1866 to 1875. Was attorney general of Tennessee from 1863 to 1865. Was named judge of the Tennessee Supreme Court in 1867 for a brief period. Was United States minister to Turkey from 1875 to 1880 and was United States postmaster general from 1880 to 1881. Maynardville, Tennessee, is named in his honor.

Green: *Lives of the Judges of the Supreme Court of Tennessee.*

MAYNARD, James (July 15, 1853—April 14, 1926)

Born in Knoxville; died in Knoxville. Was graduated from the University of Tennessee in 1872; received his LL.B. from George Washington University in 1885. Was a committee clerk for banking and currency in the United States House of Representatives from 1874 to 1875. Was a marshall to the consular courts in Turkey from 1876 to 1880. Practiced law in Knoxville, Tennessee, from 1894 to 1898. Lectured on international law at the University of Tennessee in 1897 and 1898. Was a trustee of the University of Tennessee from 1896 to 1919; was its treasurer from 1900 to 1914.

MEIGS, Return Jonathan (December 17, 1740—January 28, 1823)

Born in Middletown, Connecticut; died in the Cherokee Agency, Tennessee. Was a Revolutionary War veteran. Was a surveyor for the Ohio Company. Appointed Indian agent to the Cherokees in 1801; negotiated treaties with them in 1805 and 1807. Was given authority to negotiate between the Cherokees and the state of Tennessee.

MEIGS, Return Jonathan (April 14, 1801—October 19, 1891)

Born in Winchester, Kentucky. Was admitted to the Kentucky bar in 1822. Practiced law in Athens, Tennessee, from 1825 to 1835. Was attorney general of Tennessee from 1838 to 1839; was United States attorney for Middle Tennessee from 1841 to 1842. Served in the Tennessee Senate from 1847 to 1848. Was a Unionist during the War Between the States. Was clerk of the United States Supreme Court from 1863 to 1891. Was the author of *Code of Tennessee* and other books.

MELTON, James (January 2, 1904—April 1961)

Born in Moultrie, Georgia. Attended the Universities of Florida and

Georgia, and Vanderbilt University from 1923 to 1924. Was a radio singer in the 1920s. Traveled on concert tours after 1930. Was lead tenor for the Metropolitan Opera Company from 1942 to 1944 and from 1945 to 1952. Starred on the radio's *Texaco Star Theater* and *Telephone Hour*, as well as NBC TV's *Ford Festival* in 1951 and 1952.

MELTON, Wrightman Fletcher (September 26, 1867—November 10, 1944)

Born in Ripley, Tennessee. Was graduated from Peabody College in Nashville, Tennessee, in 1889; received his Ph.D. from Johns Hopkins University in 1906. Was vice-president of the Nashville College for Young Ladies from 1895 to 1897. Taught at numerous colleges. Was the author of *The Preacher's Son*. Was Poet Laureate of Georgia in 1943.

MENESS, Thomas (January 26, 1823—1905)

Born near Nashville, Tennessee; died in Nashville. Was a graduate of Transylvania University with a medical degree. Practiced in Springfield, Tennessee, from 1846 to 1865, and later in Nashville. Was a member of the Tennessee Senate in 1857. Served in the Confederate Congress. Was a professor at the University of Nashville from 1874 to 1875. Was dean of the medical department at Vanderbilt University from 1875 to 1896.

MERCHANT, Jane (November 1, 1919—January 3, 1972)

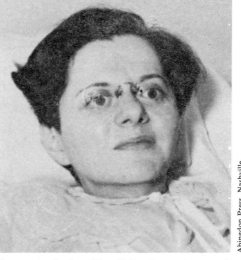

Abingdon Press, Nashville

Born in Inskip, Tennessee; buried in Knoxville, Tennessee. A bedbound invalid since childhood, and deaf at twenty-three, she never attended school but memorized Bible verses and read literary classics. She published over 2000 magazine verses and ten books (Abingdon Press at Nashville), winning many prizes and the praises of poets Carl Sandburg and Jesse Stuart. She was a traditional lyric poet with an observant eye for nature. Her superior devotional poems approach Christina Rossetti's; her better nature poems recall Robert Frost and the English Georgians of 1910-1922. She was most often compared with her favorite, Emily Dickinson. A biography and a posthumous selection of poems are projected by Abingdon Press, Nashville.

MERRITT, Dixon Lanier (July 9, 1879—January 9, 1972)

Born in Wilson County, Tennessee; died in Wilson County. Was educated locally and at the University of Nashville. Began a newspaper career at the *Nashville Banner* in 1901; worked in various news capacities until 1915. Was editor of the *Nashville Tennessee American* from 1915 to 1917. Was an editor in the office of information of the United States Department of Agriculture from 1919 to 1920. Taught journalism at Cumberland University in Lebanon, Tennessee, from 1937 on. Was the author of *History of Tennessee, Audubon in Kentucky*, and others.

MICHAUX, Andre (March 7, 1746—November 1802)

Born in Versailles, France; died in Madagascar. Explored the Tigris and Euphrates river valleys in 1782 to 1785. Came to America in 1785; to Charleston, South Carolina in 1787. Explored the Appalachian Mountains, including much of Tennessee in 1788. Returned to Paris in 1796. Was the father of Francois Andre Michaux and was the author of *Flora-Boreali Americana.*

MICHAUX, Francois Andre (August 16, 1770—October 23, 1855)

Born in Versailles, France. Came to America in 1785 with his father, Andre. Toured much of the eastern United States, including Kentucky and Tennessee, in 1801 to 1803. Visited Nashville, Knoxville, and points in between. Was the author of *Travels to the Westward of the Alleghenies.*

Thwaites: *Early Western Travels*

MILLER, Edward (?—1880)

Was a member of the James gang, participating in the robbery of a train at Glendale, Missouri, on October 7, 1879. Followed Jesse James to Tennessee after the robbery and went into a partnership with him in the purchase of a racehorse named *Jim Malone*. Sometime in the spring or summer of 1880 it is believed that Miller was killed by Jesse following an argument, possibly near Northbourne, Missouri. The disappearance of Miller, and the belief that Jesse was responsible, caused uneasiness among other gang members and ultimately contributed to Jesse's own death in 1882. (See also JAMES, Jesse Woodson.)

MILLER, Pleasant Moorman (?—1849)

Born in Lynchburg, Virginia; buried in Trenton, Tennessee. Moved to Rogersville, Tennessee, in 1796; to Knoxville, Tennessee, in 1800. Was a commissioner for Knoxville from 1801 to 1802. Served in the United States House of Representatives from 1809 to 1811. Moved to West Tennessee in 1824; was chancellor from 1836 to 1837.

MILLIGAN, Samuel (November 16, 1814—April 30, 1874)

Born in Greene County, Tennessee; died in Washington, D.C.; buried in Greeneville, Tennessee. Was a soldier in the Mexican War and a lawyer. Was a judge on the Tennessee Supreme Court from 1864 to 1868. Appointed to the United States Court of Claims in 1868.

MILLS, Clark (December 13, 1810—January 12, 1883)

Born in Onondaga, New York. Was the sculptor responsible for the identical equestrian statues of Andrew Jackson which today occupy the state capitol grounds in Nashville, Tennessee, Jackson Square in New Orleans, and Lafayette Park in Washington, D.C. At the time they were the largest bronze statues ever cast in the United States.

MIMS, Edwin (May 27, 1872—September 15, 1959)

Born in Richmond, Arkansas; died in Nashville, Tennessee; buried in Nashville. Was graduated from Vanderbilt University in 1892; received his Ph.D. from Cornell in 1900. Was assistant professor of English at Vanderbilt from 1892 to 1894; and head of Vanderbilt's English department from 1912 to 1942. Was the author of *The Advancing South* and *Life of Sidney Lanier*.

MIRO, Esteban Rodriguez (1744—1795)

Born in Catalonia, Spain. Was appointed acting Spanish governor of Louisiana in 1782; was made permanent governor in 1785. The Miro district of what later became the state of Tennessee was named in his honor. Sometimes spelled Mero, the district included Davidson, Sumner, and the old Tennessee counties. Was an advocate of the opening of the Mississippi Valley by Americans if they switched their loyalties to Spain. Conducted considerable correspondence with James Robertson at Nashville regarding this and other issues.

MITCHELL, James Coffield (March 1786—August 7, 1843)

Born in Staunton, Virginia; died near Jackson, Mississippi. Was admitted to the Virginia bar. Moved to Rhea County, Tennessee. Was solicitor general for the Second District of Tennessee from 1813 to 1817. Moved to Athens, Tennessee, in 1817. Served in the United States House of Representatives from 1825 to 1829. Was judge of the Eleventh District of Tennessee from 1830 to 1836. Moved to Hinds County, Mississippi, in 1837. Was the author of *Mitchell's Justice.*

MOON, John Austin (April 22, 1855—January 26, 1921)

Born in Albemarle County, Virginia; died in Chattanooga, Tennessee. Was educated at King College in Bristol, Tennessee. Was admitted to the Tennessee bar in 1874. Was the city attorney for Chattanooga, Tennessee, in 1881 and 1882. Was judge of the Circuit Court from 1889 to 1897. Served in the United States House of Representatives from 1897 to 1921.

MOONEY, James (February 10, 1861—December 22, 1921)

Born in Richmond, Indiana. Was educated in public schools. Began newspaper work in 1879; moved to Washington, D.C. in 1885. Became a member of the Bureau of American Ethnology of the Smithsonian Institution. Conducted studies among the Cherokee and the Great Plains Indians. Prepared the government exhibits at the Chicago, St. Louis, and Nashville expositions. In his time he was the number one authority on the Cherokee Indians. Was the author of *Myths of the Cherokees* and others.

MOORE, Delia (?—?)

Delia Moore, who used the alias Annie Rogers, was the mistress of Wild Bunch member Harvey Logan. She was arrested in the Fourth National Bank in Nashville on October 14, 1901, while attempting to exchange five hundred dollars in Montana banknotes stolen by the gang during a train robbery at Wagner, Montana, on July 3. She was brought to trial in June 1902, and acquitted of charges, largely due to a statement by Logan, who had given her the money to exchange. (See also LOGAN, Harvey.)

MOORE, Grace (December 5, 1901—January 26, 1947)

Born in Jellico, Tennessee; died in Denmark; buried in Chattanooga, Tennessee. Was educated in public schools. Studied singing under European and American masters, and sang in Irving Berlin's *Music Box Review* in 1923. Appeared professionally on Broadway and in Paris and Nice. Joined the Metropolitan Opera Company in 1928. Starred in the motion pictures *Jenny Lind* and *New Moon*, among others. Received decorations from France, Sweden, Denmark, Belgium, Cuba, and Mexico.

MOORE, John Trotwood (August 26, 1858—May 10, 1929)

Born in Marion, Alabama; died in Nashville, Tennessee. Was a graduate of Howard College in Alabama. Moved to Columbia, Tennessee, in 1885 where he raised livestock. Was editor of the *Taylor-Trotwood Magazine* from 1906 to 1911. Became director of the library, archives, and history at the Tennessee State Library in 1919. Was the author of *Ole Mistis, The Bishop of Cottontown, Tennessee—The Volunteer State,* and others.

MOORE, Merrill (September 11, 1903—September 20, 1957)

Born in Columbia, Tennessee; died in Massachusetts. Was the son of John Trotwood Moore. Attended Montgomery Bell Academy in Nashville, Tennessee, from 1916 to 1920. Was graduated from Vanderbilt University in 1924; received his M.D. degree from Vanderbilt in 1928. Was a teaching fellow at Harvard Medical School from 1930 to 1931 and a psychiatrist in the Boston area for several years. Was a World War II veteran; received the Bronze Star for action at Bougainville. Was the author of *The Noise That Time Makes, Six Sides To a Man,* and *A Doctor's Book of Hours.*

MORGAN, Harcourt A.(August 31, 1867—August 25, 1950)

Born in Adelaide Township, Ontario; died in Belfast, Tennessee. Was a pioneer in research on the cattle tick and boll weevil. Assumed the presidency of the University of Tennessee in 1919. Was elected to the Tennessee Valley Authority's first board of directors in 1933. Was elected to the Tennessee Agricultural Hall of Fame in 1951.

Makers of Millions

117

MORGAN, William Henry (February 22, 1818—1901)

Born in Logan County, Kentucky; died in Nashville, Tennessee. Was graduated from Baltimore Dental College in 1848; received his D.D. from the University of Nashville in 1871. Was president of the Tennessee Dental Association in 1867; of the American Dental Association in 1871. Was dean of the dentistry department at Vanderbilt University from 1879 to 1900. Was an Indian commissioner during Grover Cleveland's first administration.

MORRIS, John Baptist (June 29, 1866—October 22, 1947)

Born near Hendersonville, Tennessee; died in Little Rock, Arkansas. Was educated at St. Mary's College in Kentucky and at North American College in Rome, Italy. Was ordained a priest in 1892. Was pastor at St. Mary's Cathedral in Nashville, Tennessee. Was the vicar general of the diocese of Nashville from 1900 to 1906. Became bishop of Little Rock, Arkansas, in 1907. Was made assistant to the pontifical throne in 1931.

MULLINS, James (September 15, 1807—June 20, 1873)

Born in Bedford County, Tennessee; died in Shelbyville, Tennessee; buried in Shelbyville. Became a colonel in the Tennessee Militia in 1831. Was sheriff of Bedford County, Tennessee, from 1840 to 1846. Was a Union sympathizer during the War Between the States; fled from Tennessee in 1862. Served in the United States Army from 1862 to 1864. Served in the Tennessee House of Representatives in 1865; was speaker in 1865. Served in the United States House of Representatives from 1867 to 1869.

MURFREE, Mary Noailles (January 24, 1850—August 1, 1922)

Born in Murfreesboro, Tennessee; died in Murfreesboro; buried in Murfreesboro. Was the great-granddaughter of Colonel Hardy Murfree of Revolutionary War fame. She was a writer at a time when very few females wrote professionally, but concealed her identity as a woman by using the pseudonym, Charles E. Craddock. She wrote many novels with Tennessee mountain settings, including *In The Tennessee Mountains, In The Clouds,* and *The Frontiersman.*

MURFREE, William Hardy (October 2, 1781—January 19, 1827)

Born in Hertford County, North Carolina; died in Williamson County, Tennessee; buried in Williamson County. Was graduated from the University of North Carolina in 1801. Was admitted to the North Carolina bar and practiced law in Edenton. Served in the North Carolina House of Representatives from 1805 to 1812; in the United States House of Representatives from 1813 to 1817. Moved to Williamson County, Tennessee, in 1823, where he became a large landowner.

MURRELL, John A. (1804?—1846?)

Born in Williamson County, Tennessee, died in Pikeville, Tennessee; buried in Bledsoe County, Tennessee. Terrorized the old Southwest from 1826 to 1834. Was a slave stealer. Was caught in 1834 and served 10 years in the Tennessee prison in Nashville. Planned an unsuccessful slave revolt which was to occur all over the South on Christmas Day, 1835.

MYER, William Edward (October 5, 1862—December 2, 1923)

Born in Barren County, Kentucky. Moved to Carthage, Tennessee, at age six. Was educated in public schools and at age 16 entered Vanderbilt University. After graduation was offered a job as principal of a large Michigan school, which he refused. Organized the first bank in Smith County, Tennessee. Assisted in having the bridge completed across the Cumberland River at Carthage. Was an avid archaeologist and in 1919 moved to Washington, D.C., where he became associated with the Bureau of American Ethnology. Excavated several mounds and villages in Tennessee. Wrote several articles for the Bureau, including the classic *Indian Trails of the Southeast*.

N

NABERS, Benjamin Duke (November 7, 1812—September 6, 1878)

Born in Franklin, Tennessee; died in Holly Springs, Mississippi; buried in Holly Springs. Attended local schools in Tennessee; studied law. Moved to Mississippi and pursued a merchant's career. Served in the United States House of Representatives from Mississippi from 1851 to 1853. Passed the Tennessee bar in 1860; practiced law in Memphis, Tennessee. Was an elector for John Bell and the Constitutional Party in the presidential election of 1860. Settled in Holly Springs, Mississippi, in 1860; was chancery clerk from 1870 to 1874.

NASH, Francis (1742—October 7, 1777)

Born in Prince Edward County, Virginia; died in Kulpsville, Pennsylvania. Served in the North Carolina House of Commons in 1764, 1765, 1771, and from 1773 to 1775. Fought in the Battle of Alamance against the Regulators in 1771. Became a brigadier general in 1777; led a brigade at Germantown, Pennsylvania, and died in combat. Nashville, Tennessee, is named in his honor.

NEAL, John Randolph (November 26, 1836—March 26, 1889)

Born near Clinton, Tennessee; died in Rhea Springs, Tennessee; buried in Post Oak Springs, Tennessee. Attended Hiwassee College and was graduated from Emory and Henry College in 1858. Was admitted to the Tennessee bar in 1859; practiced law in Athens, Tennessee. Was a lieutenant colonel in the Confederate Army. Taught school after the war. Settled in Rhea Springs, Tennessee, and practiced law. Served in the Tennessee House of Representatives in 1874; in the Tennessee Senate from 1878 to 1879; and in the United States House of Representatives from 1885 to 1889.

NEAL, William Haskell (August 28, 1859—July 10, 1934)

Born in Wilson County, Tennessee; died in Wilson County; buried in Wilson County. Was the first man elected to the Tennessee Agricultural Hall of Fame. Was selected for his development of "Neal's Paymaster Corn." This variety, having two ears to the stalk, vastly increased production, both in Tennessee and across the United States. His research has been compared to that of the great Luther Burbank.

NEELY, Jesse (1898—April 9, 1983)

The Tennessean

Born in Smyrna, Tennessee; died in Weslaco, Texas; buried in Smyrna. Was graduated from Vanderbilt University in Nashville, Tennessee, in 1922, where he was captain of the 1922 Commodore football team. Received his law degree from Vanderbilt in 1924. He coached football at Southwestern, Alabama, and Clemson Universities. His Clemson team defeated Boston College in the 1941 Cotton Bowl. He also coached football at Rice University and later became athletic director at Vanderbilt. During his career as a head coach he compiled a 207-99-14 record and was one of only 13 head football coaches in American history to have more than 200 victories. He was a member of the National Football Hall of Fame.

NEIL, Albert Bramlett (February 28, 1873—June 26, 1966)

Born in Lewisburg, Tennessee; died in Nashville, Tennessee; buried in Nashville. Received an LL.B. from Cumberland University in 1896; was admitted to the Tennessee bar in 1896. Was criminal court judge for the Tenth Tennessee District from 1910 to 1918. Was a circuit judge from 1918 to 1942. Was dean of Cumberland University Law School from 1935 to 1940. Became a judge of the Tennessee Supreme Court in 1942, becoming chief justice in 1947 and serving until 1959.

NEIL, Matthew Marshall (1849—June 23, 1925)

Born in Fayetteville, Tennessee; died in Memphis, Tennessee. Practiced law in Trenton, Tennessee. Was president of the Tennessee Bar Association in 1892. Was a judge on the Tennessee Supreme Court from 1902 to 1918; was chief justice from 1913 to 1918.

NELSON, David (September 24, 1793—October 17, 1844)

Born in Jonesboro, Tennessee; died in Oakland, Illinois. Was graduated from Washington College in 1809. He studied medicine, and was a surgeon during the Canadian invasion and the Florida campaign during the War of 1812. Became a Presbyterian minister in 1825. Was editor of the *Calvinistic Magazine* from 1827 to 1829. Was founder and president of Marion College in Palmyra, Missouri. Was the author of *The Cause and Cure of Infidelity*.

NELSON, Thomas A. R. (March 19, 1812—1873)

Born in Roane County, Tennessee; died in Knoxville, Tennessee. Was noted as an excellent orator and lawyer. Defended Andrew Johnson in his impeachment proceedings. Was a judge of the Tennessee Supreme Court from 1870 to 1871.

NEYLAND, Robert Reese, Jr. (February 17, 1892—March 28, 1962)

Born in Greenville, Texas; died in Knoxville, Tennessee; buried in Knoxville. Was graduated from the United States Military Academy in 1916, from Massachusetts Institute of Technology in 1921. Was commissioned a second lieutenant in the United States Army in 1916. Became a brigadier general in 1944.

Johnson: *Engineers on the Twin Rivers*

121

Was professor of military tactics at the University of Tennessee from 1926 to 1931. Was head football coach from 1926 to 1934. His team lost only seven games in that period. Was district engineer on the Tennessee and Cumberland Rivers for the United States Army Corps of Engineers. Was awarded the Legion of Merit, the Distinguished Service Medal, and other service awards.

NICHOLSON, A. O. P. (August 31, 1808—March 23, 1876)

Born in Williamson County, Tennessee; died in Columbia, Tennessee. Served in the United States Senate upon Felix Grundy's death. Was offered a position in James K. Polk's cabinet, the office of postmaster general in President Pierce's administration, and the United States ministry to Spain, all of which he refused. Was a judge on the Tennessee Supreme Court from 1870 to 1876.

NIGHTINGALE, Jesse Phillip, Sr. (1919—January 23, 1981)

Born in Nashville, Tennessee; died in Nashville; buried in Nashville. Was chairman of the board of the National Baptist Publishing Board, the world's largest Black-operated religious publishing house. Was a pastor, a 32nd degree Mason, and served on the board of the Citizen's Savings Bank in Nashville, Tennessee, the oldest Black-owned financial institution in the South.

O

OCHS, Adolph S. (March 12, 1858—April 8, 1935)

Born in Cincinnati, Ohio; was educated in Knoxville, Tennessee. Attended college at Yale, Columbia, the University of Chattanooga, and New York University. Carried newspapers as a boy in Knoxville, Tennessee; later becoming owner and publisher of the *Chattanooga Times* in 1878. Became publisher and controlling owner of the *New York Times* in 1896. Was the originator of Lookout Mountain Park in Chattanooga, Tennessee.

OCHS, Julius (June 29, 1826—October 26, 1888)

Born in Furth, Germany; died in Chattanooga, Tennessee. Came to the United States in 1845. Was judge of the Knox County Court from 1868 to 1872. Became treasurer of the *Chattanooga Times* in 1878. Helped build the first bridge across the Tennessee River at Knoxville. Was the organizer of the first humane society in Chattanooga. Was a founder of Erlanger Hospital. Was the author of the opera, *The Story of Esther*.

O'CONNELL, Mary (1814—December 8, 1897)

Born in Limerick, Ireland. Was known as Sister Anthony. Attended the Ursuline Academy in Massachusetts. Served as a nurse on the battlefield of Nashville, Tennessee, during the War Between the States, and was also active at the battles of Murfreesboro, Pittsburg Landing, and others. Was recognized for her work in the yellow fever epidemic of 1877. Was known as the "Florence Nightingale of America."

OCONOSTOTA (1710—1783)

Died at Cherokee village of Echota in Tennessee. Was an eminent chief of the Cherokees. Thought to have traveled to London in 1730 as part of a group accompanied by Sir Alexander Cuming. He was originally friendly to the British, but turned against them as treaties were broken. Led the Cherokees in attacks against the whites, culminating in the Fort Loudoun massacre of 1760.

OTEY, James Hervey (January 27, 1800—April 23, 1863)

Born in Bedford County, Virginia; died in Memphis, Tennessee; buried in Maury County, Tennessee. Attended the University of North Carolina. Was appointed a deacon in the Protestant Episcopal Church in 1825; was ordained a priest in 1827. Was the founder of Harpeth Academy and St. Paul's Church, both in Franklin, Tennessee. Was the first Protestant Episcopal Bishop of Tennessee; appointed in 1833. Was a founder of the University of the South at Sewanee, Tennessee, and served as chairman of the University in 1857. Was the author of several religious works.

The Review-Appeal

OUTACITY (?—Ca. 1777)

Born in Tennessee. Was also known as the "Mankiller." Was a Cherokee Indian who took part in Oconostota's uprising in 1757. Went to England with Lieutenant Timberlake in 1762; had an audience with King George III. Fought on the side of Great Britain during the American Revolution.

OVERTON, John (April 9, 1766—April 12, 1833)

Born in Louisa County, Virginia; died in Nashville, Tennessee; buried in Nashville. Was Andrew Jackson's campaign manager for his presidential bid. Was the builder of "Traveller's Rest" near Nashville, Tennessee. Was one of the founders of Memphis, Tennessee. Was a judge of the Superior Court of Tennessee and its successor, the Supreme Court of Errors and Appeals from 1804 to 1816.

P

PAINE, Robert (November 12, 1799—October 19, 1882)

Born in Person County, North Carolina; died in Aberdeen, Mississippi. Was admitted on trial to the Tennessee Conference of the Methodist Episcopal Church in 1818; was ordained a deacon in 1821; an elder in 1823. Served as bishop from 1846 to 1882. Was a trustee of Vanderbilt University. Was the author of *Life and Times of William McKendree*.

PARKS, Edd Winfield (February 25, 1906—May 7, 1968)

Born in Newbern, Tennessee; died in Athens, Georgia. Attended the University of Tennessee from 1922 to 1923; Occidental College from 1923 to 1924. Received his bachelor's degree from Harvard in 1927; master's from Vanderbilt in 1929; Ph.D. in 1933. Was an English instructor at Vanderbilt from 1928 to 1933. Was professor of English at Cumberland University from 1933 to 1935, then taught at the University of Georgia from 1935 to 1964. Was the author of *Nashoba, Backwater, Sidney Lanier*, and other books.

PATTERSON, David Trotter (February 28, 1818—November 3, 1891)

Born in Cedar Creek, Tennessee; died in Afton, Tennessee; buried in Greeneville, Tennessee. Attended Greeneville College where he studied law. Was admitted to the Tennessee bar in 1841; practiced law in Greeneville. Was judge of the First Circuit Court of Tennessee from 1854 to 1863. Served in the United States Senate from 1866 to 1869. Had extensive agricultural interests.

PATTERSON, Malcolm (June 7, 1861—1935)

Born in Summerville, Alabama; died in Memphis, Tennessee; buried in Memphis. Served in the United States Congress. Became governor of Tennessee in 1907, serving until 1911. Was the first Tennessee governor to live in the governor's mansion; his predecessors had lived in hotels. Prohibition became a state law during his administration, but over his veto. The state guard was called out while he was governor to suppress the "Night Riders" at Reelfoot Lake.

PEARSON, Josephine (June 30, 1868—November 3, 1944)

Born in Sumner County, Tennessee; died in Nashville, Tennessee; buried in Monteagle, Tennessee. Was educated locally and in McMinnville, Tennessee. Taught in colleges in Nashville and Memphis, Tennessee; South Carolina; and Missouri. Was dean of women at Christian College in Columbia, Missouri. Was elected a leader in the anti-suffragist movement in Tennessee.

PEAY, Austin (June 1, 1876—October 2, 1927)

Born in Christian County, Kentucky; died in Nashville, Tennessee; buried in Clarksville, Tennessee. Was governor of Tennessee from 1923 to 1927. His administration is best remembered for the progress made in road construction, the assistance provided by the state in the creation of the Great Smoky Mountains National Park, and the passage of the famous anti-evolution law. Peay was the first Tennessee governor to die in office.

PECK, Jacob (Ca. 1779—June 11, 1869)

Born in Virginia; died in Jefferson County, Tennessee. Little is known about his life. Was a judge of the Tennessee Supreme Court of Errors and Appeals from 1822 to 1834.

PECK, James Hawkins (1790—April 29, 1836)

Born in Jefferson County, Tennessee; died in St. Charles, Missouri. Was a United States District Judge at St. Louis from 1818 to 1832. Was impeached, but was acquitted by the United States Congress.

PETTIBONE, Augustus Herman (January 21, 1835—November 26, 1918)

Born in Bedford, Ohio; died in Nashville, Tennessee. Was graduated from the University of Michigan in 1859. Served with the United States Army in the War Between The States. Practiced law at Greeneville, Tennessee, from 1865 to 1875; at Knoxville, Tennessee, from 1875 to 1885. Served in the United States House of Representatives from 1881 to 1887; in the Tennessee House of Representatives from 1896 to 1898. Was a special agent in the United States Land Office from 1898 to 1904.

PEYTON, Balie (November 26, 1803—August 18, 1878)

Born in Sumner County, Tennessee; died in Sumner County; buried in Sumner County. Began law practice in Gallatin, Tennessee, in 1824. Served in the United States House of Representatives from 1833 to 1837. Was United

States attorney for the Eastern District of Louisiana from 1841 to 1845. Served as United States minister to Chile from 1849 to 1853 in President Millard Filmore's administration. Was prosecuting attorney for San Francisco from 1853 to 1859. Returned to Gallatin in 1859. Served in the Tennessee Senate from 1869 to 1870.

PEYTON, Joseph Hopkins (May 20, 1808—November 11, 1845)

Born near Gallatin, Tennessee; died near Gallatin, buried near Gallatin. Was graduated from college in 1837 and was a physician. Held several government offices while practicing medicine. Served in the Tennessee Senate in 1840; in the United States House of Representatives from 1843 to 1845.

PHELAN, James (December 7, 1856—January 20, 1891)

Born in Aberdeen County, Mississippi; died in Nassau, Bahama Islands; buried in Memphis, Tennessee. Was the owner of the *Memphis Avalanche*. Was admitted to the Tennessee bar in 1881. Served in the United States House of Representatives from 1887 to 1891. Was the author of *History of Tennessee*.

PICKLE, George Wesley (March 6, 1845—?)

Born in Knoxville, Tennessee; died in Knoxville. Was a Confederate veteran. Studied at Princeton and read law at Terre Haute, Indiana, from 1868 to 1870. Was admitted to the Tennessee bar in 1870. Was attorney general of Tennessee from 1886 to 1902. Was the editor of the *Tennessee Supreme Court Reports*.

PIERCE, Rice A. (July 3, 1849—?)

Born in Weakley County, Tennessee. Was a Confederate veteran. Received his high school education in Ontario. Admitted to the Tennessee bar in 1868; practiced law in Union City in 1869. Served in the United States House of Representatives from 1883 to 1885, 1889 to 1893, and 1897 to 1905.

PILLOW, Gideon Johnson (June 8, 1806—October 8, 1878)

Born in Williamson County, Tennessee; died in Helena, Arkansas. Was graduated from the University of Nashville in 1827. Practiced law with James K. Polk in Columbia, Tennessee. Was a major general of United States volunteers in the Mexican War in 1846; served at Vera Cruz, Cerro Gordo,

126

Miller: *Photographic History of the Civil War*

and Chapultepec. Was commissioned a brigadier general in the Confederate Army in 1861; saw action at Belmont and Fort Donelson. After the war, practiced law in Memphis, Tennessee.

POLK, James Knox (November 2, 1795—June 15, 1849)

Nelson: *Sarah Childress Polk*

Born in Mecklenburg County, North Carolina; died in Nashville, Tennessee; buried in Nashville. Was graduated from the University of North Carolina in 1818. Read law under Felix Grundy. Admitted to the Tennessee bar in 1820. Was chief clerk of the Tennessee Senate from 1821 to 1823. Served in the Tennessee House of Representatives from 1823 to 1825; in the United States House of Representatives from 1825 to 1839; was speaker of the United States House from 1835 to 1839. Was governor of Tennessee from 1839 to 1841. Was president of the United States from 1845 to 1849. Was the nation's first "dark horse" president.

POLK, Leonidas (April 10, 1806—June 14, 1864)

Born in Raleigh, North Carolina; died near Marietta, Georgia. Was graduated from the United States Military Academy in 1827. Was ordained a deacon in the Episcopal Church in 1830; a priest in 1831. Was appointed the missionary bishop of the Southwest in 1838. Became bishop of Louisiana in 1841. Was responsible for the founding of the University of the South. Became a major general in the Confederate Army in 1861 and defeated Grant at Belmont. Promoted to lieutenant general in 1862. Fought

Ted Yeatman

at Shiloh, Murfreesboro, and Chickamauga, and was killed at Pine Mountain, Georgia.

POLK, Lucius Eugene (July 10, 1833—December 1, 1892)

Born in Salisbury, North Carolina; died in Maury County, Tennessee. Attended the University of Virginia. Was commissioned a brigadier general in the Confederate Army in 1862; saw action at Shiloh, Murfreesboro, Chickamauga, and Kennesaw Mountain. Served in the Tennessee Senate in 1887.

POLK, Lucius Junius (March 16, 1802—October 3, 1870)

Born in Raleigh, North Carolina; died near Ashwood, Tennessee; buried near Ashwood. The son of William Polk, Lucius came to Tennessee in 1823 to look after his father's landholdings in the state. On April 10, 1832, he married Mary Eastin, grand-niece of Rachel Jackson, at the White House, Washington, D.C., and brought her back to "Hamilton Place" in Maury County, Tennessee. Lucius represented Maury County in the Tennessee Senate, 1831-1833, and served as adjutant-general of Tennessee, 1851-1853. With his brothers Rufus K., George Washington, and Leonidas, he helped found St. John's Episcopal Church in 1842, near Ashwood, in Maury County. (See also POLK, Leonidas and POLK, William.)

Ted Yeatman

POLK, Sarah Childress (September 4, 1803—August 14, 1891)

Born in Rutherford County, Tennessee; died in Nashville, Tennessee; buried in Nashville. Was educated by Moravians. Married James K. Polk on January 1, 1824. Prohibited dancing and drinking at the White House while she was first lady. Lived in Nashville at Polk Place for many years after her husband's death and was highly regarded by all who knew her.

Nelson: Sarah Childress Polk

128

POLK, William (July 9, 1758—January 14, 1834)

Born near Charlotte, North Carolina; died in Raleigh, North Carolina; buried in Raleigh. Was an officer in the American Revolution. Was appointed surveyor general in 1783 of the portion of North Carolina which later became Tennessee. He represented Davidson County in the North Carolina House of Commons from 1785 to 1787 and served as a trustee of Davidson Academy, later to become George Peabody College, during the same period. He acquired large land holdings in Tennessee, some of which were passed on to his sons Leonidas and Lucius. (See also: POLK, Leonidas and POLK, Lucius Junius.)

Ted Yeatman

POLK, William Hawkins (May 24, 1815—December 16, 1862)

Born in Maury County, Tennessee; died in Nashville, Tennessee; buried in Columbia, Tennessee. Attended the University of North Carolina; was graduated from the University of Tennessee. Admitted to the Tennessee bar in 1839; practiced in Columbia, Tennessee. Served in the Tennessee House of Representatives from 1842 to 1845. Was United States minister to the Kingdom of Naples from 1845 to 1847. Served in the United States House of Representatives from 1851 to 1853.

PORTER, Alexander (1786—January 13, 1844)

Born in County Donegal, Ireland; died in Attakapas, Louisiana; buried in Louisiana. Came to the United States in 1801. Was admitted to the Tennessee bar in 1807. Moved to Louisiana and served in the Louisiana House of Representatives from 1816 to 1818. Was an associate judge of the Louisiana Supreme Court from 1821 to 1833. Served in the United States Senate from 1833 to 1837. Was a large land owner in Louisiana.

PORTER, James D. (December 7, 1828—May 18, 1912)

Born in Paris, Tennessee; died in Paris, buried in Paris. A lawyer by profession, Porter served as General Gideon Pillow's adjutant and General Benjamin Cheatham's chief of staff during the War Between the States. Was governor of Tennessee from 1875 to 1879. Afterwards, he was president of the Nashville, Chattanooga, and St. Louis Railroad, and was United States secretary of state under Grover Cleveland, and United States minister to Chile. Porter was asked to run for the presidency of the United States, but refused.

PORTER, William Sydney "O. Henry" (September 11, 1862—June 5, 1910)

Dictionary of American Portraits

Born in Greensboro, North Carolina; buried in Asheville, North Carolina. Was a popular magazine storyteller in the first years of the twentieth century. In 1905 his daughter Margaret began attending Ward-Belmont finishing school in Nashville, Tennessee. A visit to the city gave O. Henry background for one of his best short stories, "A Municipal Report," written in 1909 in New York City. Nashville is unflatteringly described: "Take of London fog 30 parts; malaria 10 parts; gas leaks 20 parts; dewdrops gathered in a brick yard at sunrise, 25 parts; odor of honey suckle 15 parts. Mix." One scene is set at the Maxwell House, and tarnished antebellum characters (or caricatures) are bitingly demythologized. The tale has been acclaimed as one of America's great short stories; contemporary reaction in Nashville was markedly more restrained.

POWEL, Samuel (July 10, 1776—August 2, 1841)

Born in Norristown, Pennsylvania; died in Rogersville, Tennessee. Was judge of the Tennessee Superior Court from 1807 to 1810. Powel County, Tennessee (later abolished) was named in his honor.

PRESLEY, Elvis Aaron (January 8, 1935—August 16, 1977)

Born in Tupelo, Mississippi; died in Memphis, Tennessee; buried in Memphis. Moved to Memphis, Tennessee, at age 13. Sang for dances; appeared on the Louisiana Hayride Program in 1955. Pursued "rockabilly bluegrass" music at

Hank Snow

first, then "rock and roll." His appearance on the *Ed Sullivan Show* pushed him into national prominence. His records have sold millions.

PRIEST, James Percy (April 1, 1900—October 12, 1956)

Born in Carter's Creek community, Tennessee; buried in Nashville, Tennessee. Attended Middle Tennessee State College, the University of Tennessee, and Peabody College. Was a teacher in Maury County, Tennessee. Taught at Culleoka High School from 1921 to 1926. Was a newspaperman in Nashville, Tennessee, from 1926 to 1940. Served in the United States House of Representatives in the Seventy-eighth through the Eighty-fourth Congresses.

PRIESTLEY, James (?—February 6, 1821)

Born in Rockbridge County, Virginia; died in Nashville, Tennessee. Was principal at Salem Academy in Bardstown, Kentucky, from 1788 to 1792; principal of the male department of Baltimore Academy from 1796 to 1798; principal of Cumberland College (University of Nashville) from 1809 to 1816 and from 1820 to 1821.

PRYOR, James Charles (March 13, 1871—September 8, 1947)

Born in Winchester, Tennessee; died in New York; buried in Arlington, Virginia. Was graduated from the University of Nashville; received an M.D. from Vanderbilt University. Was graduated from the United States Army College in 1928. Entered the Navy as an ensign in 1897; obtained the rank of rear admiral in 1934. Served in the Spanish-American War. Was medical attendant to Theodore Roosevelt at the White House. Was commander of the United States Navy hospitals at Yokahama, Pensacola, and Hampton Roads, Virginia. Was the author of *Naval Hygiene*.

PUTNAM, Albigence Waldo (March 11, 1799—January 20, 1869)

Born in Belpre, Ohio; died in Nashville, Tennessee; buried in Nashville. Was educated at Ohio University; was graduated in 1820 and admitted to the Ohio bar. Moved to Port Gibson, Mississippi, where he practiced law. Moved back to Ohio, then to Nashville, Tennessee. Was active in revitalizing the Tennessee Historical Society in 1849; was its vice-president until 1857, then its president. Was the author of *History of Middle Tennessee*.

Q

QUINTARD, Charles Todd (December 22, 1824—February 15, 1898)

Born in Stamford, Connecticut. Received his M.D. from New York University in 1847. Was professor at Memphis Medical College in 1851. Was ordained a deacon in the Episcopal Church in 1855. Was chaplain for the Confederate States of America. Was bishop of Tennessee from 1865 to 1898. Was a founder of the University of the South; managed it until 1872.

R

RAMSEY, James Gettys McGready (March 25, 1797—April 11, 1884)

East Tennessee Historical Society

Born near Knoxville, Tennessee; died in Knoxville; buried in Knoxville. Was graduated from Washington College in Tennessee in 1816, then studied medicine at the University of Pennsylvania and began his practice in Knoxville in 1820. Was a director of the Louisville, Cincinnati, and Charleston Railroad, and was president of a bank in Knoxville. Served as president of the Tennessee Historical Society from 1874 to 1884 and wrote *Annals of Tennessee to the End of the 18th Century.*

RAYBURN, Sam (January 6, 1882—November 16, 1961)

Born in Roane County, Tennessee; buried in Bonham, Texas. Moved to Texas at a young age. Was graduated from East Texas College, then studied law at the University of Texas. Served six years (two years as speaker) in the Texas House of Representatives. Served in the United States House of Representatives from the Sixty-third through the Eighty-seventh Congresses; was speaker during the Seventy-seventh through the Seventy-ninth, the Eighty-first, and the Eighty-second through the Eighty-seventh Congresses. Was the permanent chairman of the Democratic National Convention in 1952 and 1956.

READ, Opie (December 22, 1852—November 2, 1939)

Born in Nashville, Tennessee. Was educated in Gallatin, Tennessee. Began a

132

newspaper career in Franklin, Kentucky, then Little Rock, Arkansas. Was editor of the *Arkansas Gazette* from 1878 to 1881. Was on the staff of the *Cleveland (Ohio) Leader* from 1881 to 1883. Was the author of *A Tennessee Judge, In The Alamo*, and *An American in New York*, among many other novels.

READY, Charles (December 22, 1802—June 4, 1878)

Born in Readyville, Tennessee; died in Murfreesboro, Tennessee; buried in Murfreesboro. Was graduated from Greeneville College and was admitted to the Tennessee bar in 1825. He practiced law in Murfreesboro, Tennessee, and served in the Tennessee House of Representatives in 1835, and in the United States House of Representatives from 1853 to 1859.

REAGAN, John Henninger (October 8, 1818—1905)

Born in Sevier County, Tennessee; died in Texas. Was educated locally. Attended Maryville College (Tennessee). Moved to the Republic of Texas where he fought Indians. Was deputy surveyor of public lands from 1839 to 1844. Began a law practice in 1846; was elected to the Texas Legislature in 1847. Served in the United States House of Representatives from 1857 to 1861. Was a member of the Confederate Provisional Congress. Was postmaster general of the Confederacy from 1861 to 1865. Served in the United States House of Representatives from 1875 to 1887. Was United States senator from 1887 to 1891.

Harper's Pictorial History of the Civil War

REECE, William Brown (November 19, 1793—July 7, 1859)

Born in Jefferson County, Tennessee; died in Knoxville, Tennessee; buried in Knoxville. Was a judge of the Tennessee Supreme Court from 1835 to 1847. Afterwards he ran as a Whig for the United States Senate, but was defeated by John Bell. In 1850 he became president of East Tennessee University, today's University of Tennessee.

REED, Forrest Francis (September 11, 1897—March 22, 1975)

Born in Fulton, Mississippi; died in Nashville, Tennessee; buried in

Nashville, Tennessee. Was organizer and president of Tennessee Book Company in Nashville, Tennessee. Owned Reed and Company, a publishing firm in Nashville, from 1965 to 1975. Was the president of the Tennessee Convention of Christian Churches in 1957. Was a member of the Disciples of Christ Historical Society from 1952 to 1975.

REEVES, James Travis "Jim" (August 20, 1923—July 31, 1964)

Les Leverett

Born in Galloway, Texas; died in Davidson County, Tennessee; buried in Carthage, Texas. Acquired a guitar at age 5; made his first radio broadcast at age 9. Signed a contract with the St. Louis Cardinals baseball club, but an injury ended his baseball career. Was a disc jockey and newscaster in Henderson, Texas. In 1952, he filled in for Hank Williams on the Louisiana Hayride and was immediately offered a contract. Recorded *Mexican Joe* in 1953. In 1955, he joined the Grand Ole Opry. Was killed in an airplane accident. Was admitted to the Country Music Hall of Fame in 1967.

REYNOLDS, James B. (1779—June 10, 1851)

Born in County Antrim, Ireland; died in Clarksville, Tennessee; buried in Clarksville. Attended common schools; studied law. Came to the United States and settled in Clarksville, Tennessee. Admitted to the Tennessee bar in 1804. Served in the United States House of Representatives from 1815 to 1817 and from 1823 to 1825.

RHEA, JOHN (1753—May 27, 1832)

Born in County Donegal, Ireland; died in Blountville, Tennessee. Came to the United States in 1769. Served in the North Carolina House of Commons from 1785 to 1790. Was an incorporator of Washington College in Greeneville, Tennessee, and of the University of

Taylor: *Historic Sullivan*

134

Tennessee. Was a delegate to the first Tennessee Constitutional Convention in 1796. Served in the Tennessee legislature in 1796 and 1797. Served in the United States House of Representatives from 1803 to 1815 and from 1817 to 1823. Rhea County, Tennessee, is named in his honor.

RICE, Grantland (November 1, 1880—July 13, 1954)

Born in Murfreesboro, Tennessee; buried in New York. Attended school in Nashville, Tennessee. Received his B.A. from Vanderbilt University in 1901. Was a journalist with the *Nashville News,* the *Atlanta Journal*, the *Cleveland News,* the *Nashville Tennessean,* the *New York Mail,* and the *New York Tribune.* Wrote the *Sportlight*, a syndicated column from 1930 till his death. Was the president of Grantland Rice Sportlights, Inc., a movie company. Was the author of *Songs of the Stalwart* and *Only The Brave.*

RICHARDSON, James Daniel (March 10, 1843—1914)

Born in Rutherford County, Tennessee; died in Murfreesboro, Tennessee. Left Franklin College before graduation to join the Confederate Army. Began law practice at Murfreesboro, Tennessee, in 1867. Served in the Tennessee House of Representatives from 1871 to 1872; Tennessee Senate from 1873 to 1874. Was chairman of the Democratic National Convention in 1900. Served in the United States House of Representatives. Was the editor of *Messages and Papers of the Presidents* and *Messages and Papers of the Confederacy.*

RIDDLE, Haywood Yancey (1834—March 28, 1879)

Born in Hardeman County, Tennessee; died in Lebanon, Tennessee; buried in Lebanon. Was graduated from Union University in Murfreesboro, Tennessee, in 1854; from Cumberland University Law School in 1857. Taught math and languages at Union University; was a Confederate veteran. Moved to Lebanon, Tennessee, in 1865. Served in the United States House of Representatives from 1875 to 1879.

RITTER, Woodward Maurice "Tex" (January 12, 1905—January 2, 1973)

Born in Panola County, Texas; died in Nashville, Tennessee. Aspired to a law profession. Played on Broadway in the 1930s. Followed Gene Autry onto the movie screen

135

as a singing cowboy. Moved to Hollywood in 1936; played in 60 films. Was one of country music's biggest sellers in the 1940s. Moved to Nashville, Tennessee, in 1965. Performed on the Grand Ole Opry. Ran for the United States Senate in 1970. Was instrumental in establishing the Country Music Hall of Fame. Was elected to same in 1964.

RIVERS, Thomas (September 18, 1819—March 18, 1863)

Born in Franklin County, Tennessee; died in Somerville, Tennessee; buried in Somerville. Attended La Grange College in Alabama. Admitted to the Tennessee bar in 1839; practiced law in Somerville, Tennessee. Was a brigadier general in the Tennessee Militia. Served in the United States House of Representatives from 1855 to 1857.

ROANE, Archibald (1760—January 18, 1819)

Born in Dauphin County, Pennsylvania; died in Knox County, Tennessee; buried in Campbell's Station, Tennessee. Was a lawyer by profession. Fought conspicuously in the Continental Army during the Revolution. Assisted in framing Tennessee's first constitution in 1796. Served as governor of Tennessee from 1801 to 1803. Under his guidance as governor, Tennessee grew in size to merit three congressional districts. Roane County, Tennessee, is named in his honor.

Green: Lives of the Judges of the Supreme Court of Tennessee

ROBBINS, Marty

See ROBINSON, Martin David.

ROBERTS, Albert H. (July 4, 1868—June 25, 1946)

Born in Overton County, Tennessee; died near Nashville, Tennessee; buried in Livingston, Tennessee. Was a school teacher and a lawyer. Was governor of Tennessee from 1919 to 1921. Important achievements of his administration included the passage of the law allowing women to vote and a workmen's compensation law.

ROBERTS, Issachar Jacob (February 17, 1802—December 28, 1871)

Born in Sumner County, Tennessee; died in Upper Alton, Illinois. Attended Furman Theological Institute. Was the organizer of the Roberts Fund and China Mission Society; arrived in China in 1837. Opened a Baptist mission in Hong Kong in 1842. Was minister of foreign affairs for the Chinese rebels in 1862; returned to the United States in 1866.

ROBERTSON, Charlotte Reeves (January 2, 1751—June 11, 1843)

Born in North Hampton County, North Carolina; died in Nashville, Tennessee; buried in Nashville. Joined her husband James Robertson, in the settlement of Nashville, Tennessee. Gave birth to the first white child in the Cumberland settlements. Was the heroine of the Battle of the Bluffs in April 1781, when she unleashed a pack of dogs upon the Indian attackers who had ambushed the fort's men outside the stockade. Charlotte, Tennessee, is named in her honor.

ROBERTSON, Edward White (June 13, 1823—August 2, 1887)

Born near Nashville, Tennessee; died in Baton Rouge, Louisiana; buried in Baton Rouge. Attended Augusta College in Kentucky. Studied law at the University of Nashville; was graduated with a law degree from the University of Louisiana in 1850. Was a Mexican War veteran. Served in the Louisiana House of Representatives from 1847 to 1849 and in 1853. Was a Confederate veteran. Served in the United States House of Representatives from Louisiana from 1877 to 1883 and in 1887.

ROBERTSON, Felix (January 11, 1781—July 10, 1865)

Born in Nashville, Tennessee; died in Nashville, buried in Nashville. Was the first white child born in Nashville, Tennessee. Attended Davidson Academy. Opened a medical practice in Nashville in 1806 after graduation from the University of Pennsylvania. Became the mayor of Nashville in 1827. Was president of the Bank of Tennessee. Was a charter member of the Medical Society of Tennessee and was its president in 1834.

Tennessee Historical Society

ROBERTSON, Harrison (January 16, 1856—November 11, 1939)

Born in Murfreesboro, Tennessee; died in Louisville, Kentucky. Was educated at Union University and the University of Virginia. Was on the staff of the *Louisville Courier-Journal* from 1879; was columnist, literary critic, and chief editorial writer. Was editor-in-chief from 1929. Was the author of *How The Derby Was Won*, *The Pink Typhoon*, and others.

ROBERTSON, James (June 28, 1742—September 1, 1814)

Born in Brunswick County, Virginia; died in the Chickasaw Agency, West Tennessee; buried in Nashville, Tennessee. Crossed the Blue Ridge Mountains with Daniel Boone in 1769 and was a founder of the Watauga settlements in East Tennessee. Defended Watauga against the Indians in 1777. Moved to the Cumberland River Valley and founded Nashville, Tennessee, in 1779. Was a trustee of Davidson Academy in 1785. Led the Coldwater Expedition against the Indians in 1787. Was brigadier general for the Southwest Territory until 1794. Served in the Tennessee Senate in 1798. Often called the "Father of Tennessee."

ROBINSON, Martin David "Marty Robbins" (September 26, 1925—December 8, 1982)

Les Leverett

Born in Glendale, Arizona; died in Nashville, Tennessee; buried in Nashville. Served in the United States Navy. Under the influence of Gene Autry, he realized his ambition to become a "singing cowboy." He played in clubs in the Phoenix, Arizona area. Upon the recommendation of Little Jimmy Dickens, he became a Grand Ole Opry regular in 1953, and became famous for his cowboy and Mexican-style ballads. He was elected to the Country Music Hall of Fame in 1982, and was a two-time Grammy Award winner. He was also an accomplished stock car racer.

ROGAN, Hugh (September 16, 1747—1814)

Born in County Donegal, Ireland; died in Sumner County, Tennessee;

buried in Sumner County. Visited Sumner County, Tennessee, in 1779 with a state line survey party. Returned to the Cumberland Valley with John Donelson in 1780. Returned to Ireland in 1796 and brought his wife and 22-year-old son to Sumner County. Was granted 640 acres near today's Vanderbilt University in Nashville, Tennessee, and traded it for Sumner County land. Built his stone and brick house, *Rogana*, in 1800 in Sumner County.

ROGERS, Annie

See MOORE, Delia.

ROSE, Fred (August 24, 1897—December 1, 1954)

Born in Evansville, Indiana; died in Nashville, Tennessee; buried in Nashville. Was the founder of Acuff-Rose Music Company. Was a songwriter; wrote *Blue Eyes Crying in the Rain, Kaw-Liga, Take These Chains From My Heart*. Wrote for Sophie Tucker and with Gene Autry. Established a music company in Nashville, Tennessee, in 1942. Helped break the hold of New York City publishers on the music industry. Became one of the first members of the Country Music Hall of Fame.

ROSE, Wickliffe (November 19, 1862—September 5, 1931)

Born in Saulsbury, Tennessee; died in New York City. Was graduated from the University of Nashville in 1889; received his LL.D. from the University of Mississippi in 1910. Was an instructor of history and math at Peabody College in Nashville, Tennessee, in 1891 and 1892; professor of philosophy at Peabody from 1892 to 1902. Was professor of history and philosophy at the University of Tennessee from 1902 to 1904. Was dean of Peabody from 1904 to 1907. Was a member of the Rockefeller Foundation.

ROSS, John (October 3, 1790—August 1, 1866)

Born near Lookout Mountain, Tennessee; died in Washington, D.C. Was the adjutant of a Cherokee Indian regiment in Andrew Jackson's army during the Creek Wars from 1812 to 1814. Became a member of the National Council of Cherokees in 1817; was its president from 1819 to 1826.

McKenney and Hall: *Indian Tribes of North America*

Helped draft the Cherokee constitution in 1827. Was elected principal chief of the eastern Cherokees in 1828 and served until 1839. He was opposed to the removal, but finally led his tribe to Oklahoma in 1838 and 1839. United the eastern and western branches of the Cherokees and was chief of the United Cherokee Nation from 1839 to 1866.

ROSS, John William (?—July 9, 1925)

Born in Hardin County, Tennessee. Was educated at Southern Normal University in Huntingdon, Tennessee, and Cumberland University at Lebanon, Tennessee. Received his LL.B. from Cumberland in 1900. Practiced law at Savannah, Tennessee, from 1900 to 1913. Was chancellor of the Eighth Chancery District of Tennessee from 1913 to 1921. Was judge of the United States District Court, Western Division, from 1921 to 1925.

ROULSTONE, George (October 8, 1767—1804)

Born in Boston, Massachusetts; died in Knoxville, Tennessee. Was the founder and publisher of Tennessee's first newspaper, the *Knoxville Gazette*, from 1791 to 1804. Was the official printer for the Southwest Territory from 1791 to 1796. Was the official printer for the state of Tennessee from 1796 to 1804. Was the postmaster of Knoxville, a city commissioner, and a trustee for Blount College (today's University of Tennessee).

RULE, William (May 10, 1839—July 25, 1928)

Born in Knox County, Tennessee; died in Knoxville, Tennessee. Was a private and an officer in the United States Army during the War Between the States. Was editor of the *Knoxville Chronicle* from 1870 to 1882. Became editor of the *Knoxville Daily Journal and Tribune* in 1885. Was postmaster of Knoxville for two terms and mayor of Knoxville for two terms. Was a trustee for the University of Tennessee and the secretary of its board of trustees for 40 years.

RUTHERFORD, Griffith (1721—August 10, 1805)

Born in Scotland; died in Wilson County, Tennessee. Moved to America in 1739. Was a surveyor in Halifax County, North Carolina. Was sheriff of Rowan County, North Carolina, in 1769. Was appointed a brigadier general of the North Carolina Militia in 1776. Moved to Washington County, in what is now Tennessee, then to Sumner County, then to Wilson County. Rutherford counties in North Carolina and Tennessee are named in his honor.

RYAN, William (Ca. 1851—?)

As a member of the Jesse James gang (See JAMES, Jesse Woodson), Ryan took part in a train robbery at Glendale, Missouri, on October 8, 1879. In 1880 he accompanied Jesse James to Tennessee and participated in robberies at Mammoth Cave, Kentucky, on September 3, 1880, and Muscle Shoals, Alabama, on March 11, 1881. Ryan was captured at Whites Creek, Tennessee, on March 25, 1881, and returned to Missouri for trial. According to one source, his conviction "...broke the back of outlawry in the state of Missouri...." Released from prison in 1889, he was reportedly living as late as 1898, whence he disappears from the pages of history.

RYE, Thomas C. (1863—September 12, 1953)

Born in Camden, Tennessee; buried in Paris, Tennessee. Was district attorney in Paris, Tennessee. Was governor of Tennessee from 1915 to 1919. He was a hard-hitting prohibitionist, and his administration is best remembered for its passage of the Ouster Law, whereby unworthy public officials could be turned out of office. The first casualty of the law was Memphis mayor E. H. (Boss) Crump.

S

SAFFORD, James Merrill (August 13, 1822—1907)

Born in Zanesville, Ohio; died in Dallas, Texas. Was graduated from Ohio University in 1844; received a Ph.D. from Yale in 1866; received his M.D. degree from the University of Nashville in 1872. Was professor of natural science at Cumberland University from 1848 to 1872. Was professor of chemistry and medicine at the University of Nashville and at Vanderbilt University from 1874 to 1894. Was state geologist for Tennessee from 1854 to 1860 and from 1871 to 1900. Was the author of *Geology of Tennessee*.

SANFORD, Edward Terry (July 23, 1865—March 8, 1930)

Born in Knoxville, Tennessee; died in Washington, D.C. Was graduated from the University of Tennessee in 1883; completed post-graduate work at Harvard in 1885; received his LL.D. from the University of Cincinnati in 1908. Was admitted to the Tennessee bar in 1888. Was assistant attorney general of the United States from 1907 to 1908. Was United States district judge for the eastern and middle district of Tennessee from 1908 to 1923. Became an associate justice of the United States Supreme Court in 1923.

SANFORD, James T. (?—?)

Born in Virginia. Moved to Columbia, Tennessee; was a farmer. Served in the United States House of Representatives from 1823 to 1825. Assisted in the organization of Jackson College at Columbia, Tennessee.

SAPPINGTON, John (May 15, 1776—September 7, 1856)

Born in Maryland. Attended the University of Pennsylvania. Moved to Nashville, Tennessee. Was a commissioner who assisted in the formulation of the town plan of Franklin, Tennessee, in 1799. Moved to Missouri in 1817. Was an advocate for the use of quinine in the treatment of malaria. Was the originator of "Dr. Sappington's Anti-Fever Pills" in 1832. Wrote the first medical book to be published west of the Mississippi River, *Theory and Treatment of Fevers*, published in 1844.

Jim Farrell; Crutchfield: *Footprints Across the Pages of Tennessee History*

SAVAGE, George Martin (February 5, 1849—June 1938)

Born in Tishomingo County, Mississippi; died in Jackson, Tennessee. Received a degree from Southwestern Baptist University in 1871; received his LL.D. in 1890. Was ordained a Baptist minister in 1870. Taught at Southwestern Baptist University from 1877 to 1880. Was principal at Eagleville (Tennessee) High School from 1884 to 1890. Was president of Southwestern Baptist University from 1890 to 1904, from 1906 to 1907, and from 1915 to 1918.

SAVAGE, Giles Christopher (January 15, 1854—?)

Born near Rienzi, Mississippi; died in Nashville, Tennessee. Was educated in Mississippi and at the Masonic Institute at Henderson, Tennessee. Received an M.D. degree from Jefferson Medical College in Philadelphia in 1878. Performed postgraduate work in London and Vienna. Practiced medicine in Jackson, Tennessee, from 1878 to 1886; in Nashville, Tennessee, from 1886 onwards. Was professor of ophthalmology at Vanderbilt University from 1886 to 1911. Was president of the Nashville Academy of Medicine from 1891 to 1892; of the Tennessee Medical Association in 1896. Was the author of *New Truths in Ophthalmology*.

SAVAGE, John H. (October 9, 1815—April 5, 1904)

Born in McMinnville, Tennessee; died in McMinnville. Attended Carroll Academy in McMinnville, Tennessee. Was admitted to the Tennessee bar in 1839; practiced in Smithville, Tennessee. Was a veteran of the Seminole and Mexican wars, as well as the War Between the States. Was attorney general of Tennessee from 1842 to 1847. Served in the United States House of Representatives from 1849 to 1853 and from 1855 to 1859. Served in the Tennessee legislature during the sessions of 1877, 1879, and 1887.

SAWYER, Frederick Adolphus (December 12, 1822—July 31, 1891)

Born in Bolton, Massachusetts; died in Claiborne County, Tennessee; buried near East Cumberland Gap, Tennessee. Was graduated from Harvard University in 1844. Served in the United States Senate from South Carolina from 1868 to 1873. Was assistant secretary of the United States Treasury from 1873 to 1874. Moved to Tennessee; became president of a land company at Cumberland Gap, Tennessee. Died suddenly in a hotel in Shawnee, Tennessee.

SCARBOROUGH, William Harrison (November 7, 1812—August 16, 1871)

Born in Dover, Tennessee; died in Columbia, South Carolina. Studied medicine and art in Cincinnati. Worked as a portrait painter in Tennessee. Moved to South Carolina in 1830; to Columbia, South Carolina in 1843. Was a successful portrait artist and painter in North and South Carolina.

SCOTT, Robert Nicholson (January 21, 1838—March 5, 1887)

Born in Winchester, Tennessee; died in Washington, D.C. Was a major in the United States Army in 1862; was senior aide to General Halleck from 1863 to 1864. Was commander of Ft. Ontario, New York, from 1873 to 1877. Was a member of a committee to reorganize the United States Army from 1877 to 1887. Was the author of *Digest of the Military Laws of the U.S.*

SCOTT, William Anderson (January 31, 1813—January 14, 1885)

Born in Bedford County, Tennessee; died in San Francisco. Was graduated from Cumberland College in Kentucky in 1833. Attended Princeton University and the University of Alabama. Was licensed to preach in 1830 and became a missionary in Louisiana and Arkansas in 1835 and 1836. Was president of the Nashville Female Seminary from 1838 to 1840. Preached in New

York City and San Francisco and was a founder of City College in San Francisco. Was the author of *The Giant Judges*.

SEBASTIAN, William King (1812—May 20, 1865)

Born in Hickman County, Tennessee; died in Memphis, Tennessee; buried in Helena, Arkansas. Was graduated from Columbia College in Columbia, Tennessee. Practiced law in Helena, Arkansas, in 1835 and raised cotton. Served as circuit judge from 1840 to 1843. Was an associate justice of the Arkansas Supreme Court from 1843 to 1845. Was president of the Arkansas Senate in 1846 and 1847. Served in the United States Senate from 1848 to 1861. Practiced law in Helena during the War Between the States. Moved to Memphis, Tennessee, after the Union occupation of Helena.

SENTER, De Witt Clinton (1834—June 14, 1898)

Born in McMinn County, Tennessee; died in Morristown, Tennessee; buried in Morristown. Was speaker of the Tennessee Senate when Governor Brownlow was elected to the United States Senate. Senter thus became the second Tennessee governor to gain the governor's chair through succession, serving from 1869 to 1871. He governed during hard times, with mass poverty, mistrust, and a carpetbagging mentality dominating the scene.

SENTER, William Tandy (May 12, 1801—August 28, 1848)

Born in Bean Station, Tennessee; died in Hamblen County, Tennessee. Was a local office holder and a farmer, as well as a Methodist minister. Was a member of the Tennessee Constitutional Convention of 1834 and then served in the United States House of Representatives from 1843 to 1845.

SEQUOYAH "George Guess" or "Gist" (1760—1843)

Born in Monroe County, Tennessee; died in Mexico. Raised in the Cherokee Nation. After a hunting accident he devoted himself to inventing a Cherokee alphabet of 85 characters, which enabled Cherokee speakers to learn to read and write. He died while traveling in Mexico to verify the story that some Cherokees lived there. Sequoia National Park and a genus of trees,

McKenney and Hall: *Indian Tribes of North America.*

Sequoia, are named for him. Took the name George Guess from the white trader he believed was his father.

SEVIER, Ambrose Hundley (November 10, 1801—December 31, 1848)

Born in Greene County, Tennessee; died in Pulaski County, Arkansas; buried near Little Rock, Arkansas. Moved to Arkansas in 1821. Was clerk of the Arkansas Territorial House of Representatives in 1821. Was a member of the Arkansas Territorial House of Representatives from 1823 to 1827; was speaker in 1827. Was a delegate to the United States Congress from Arkansas Territory from 1828 to 1836. Served in the United States Senate from Arkansas from 1836 to 1848. Was United States minister to Mexico in 1848.

SEVIER, John (September 23, 1745—September 24, 1815)

Born in Rockingham County, Virginia; died in Alabama; buried in Knoxville, Tennessee. Was a soldier, Indian fighter, state senator, and United States congressman at one time or another. Was governor of the "Lost" State of Franklin from 1784 to 1788. Was governor of Tennessee from 1796 to 1801 and from 1803 to 1809. Sevier County, Tennessee, is named in his honor.

Tennessee State Museum

SHACKLEFORD, James O. (1809—1880)

Born in Nashville, Tennessee; died in Denver, Colorado. Was appointed a judge of the Tennessee Supreme Court by Governor William Brownlow. His term is uncertain, probably from 1865 to 1869 with part of 1868 vacated. Practiced law in Nashville after retiring from the bench and then moved to Colorado for his health.

SHARKEY, William Lewis (July 12, 1798—March 30, 1873)

Born in Sumner County, Tennessee; died in Washington, D.C.; buried in Jackson, Mississippi. Was admitted to the Mississippi bar in 1822. Served in the Mississippi House of Representatives from 1828 to 1829. Was chief justice of the Mississippi High Court of Errors and Appeals from 1832 to 1857. Was president of the Nashville Convention in 1850. Was an anti-secessionist during the War Between the States. Was provisional governor of

Mississippi in 1865. Was elected to the United States Senate in 1866, but was denied his seat.

SHELBY, Evan (1719—December 4, 1794)

Born in Wales; died in Bristol, Tennessee; buried in Bristol. Came to America in 1734; settled in Maryland. Fought in the French and Indian War. Moved to Virginia in 1773. Was a colonel in the Washington (Virginia) Militia in 1776. Led 2,000 men against the Chickamauga Indian towns on the Tennessee River in 1779. Served in the North Carolina Senate in 1781. Was brigadier general in the Washington District (North Carolina) Militia from 1786 to 1787. Refused the position as governor of the "Lost" State of Franklin.

SHELBY, Isaac (December 11, 1750—July 18, 1826)

Born in Washington County, Maryland; died near Stanford, Kentucky. Fought at the Battle of Point Pleasant in 1774. Attended the Long Island Treaty meeting with the Cherokees. Served in the Virginia legislature in 1779. Was a colonel in the Sullivan County (North Carolina) Militia in 1780. Served in the North Carolina legislature in 1781. Was the first governor of Kentucky from 1792 to 1796 and then served again from 1812 to 1816. Appointed with Andrew Jackson to treaty with the Chickasaws for the land in Tennessee west of the Tennessee River. Shelby County, Tennessee, and the Shelby counties in eight other states are named in his honor.

SHELBY, John (May 24, 1785—May 15, 1859)

Born in Sumner County, Tennessee; died in Nashville, Tennessee; buried in Nashville. Was the first white child born in the area which became Sumner County, Tennessee. Was a physician by profession. Founded the Shelby Medical College which later merged with the University of Nashville Medical School. Promoted the erection of the first suspension bridge over the Cumberland River at Nashville. Was a veteran of the War of 1812. Helped establish St. Ann's Episcopal Church in Nashville and was a large landowner in East Nashville. Shelby Park, Avenue, and Bridge in Nashville are named in his honor.

SHIELDS, Ebenezer J. (December 22, 1778—April 21, 1846)

Born in Georgia; died near LaGrange, Texas. Was graduated from the University of Nashville in 1827. Was admitted to the Tennessee bar and practiced law in Pulaski, Tennessee. Served in the Tennessee House of Representatives from 1833 to 1835; in the United States House of Representatives from 1835 to 1839. Moved to Memphis, Tennessee, in 1844 and continued his law practice there.

SHIELDS, John K. (August 15, 1858—September 30, 1934)

Born in Grainger County, Tennessee; died in Grainger County; buried in Grainger County. Served as a judge of the Tennessee Supreme Court from 1902 to 1913; was chief justice from 1910 to 1913. Afterwards, served in the United States Senate from 1913 to 1925.

SHIPP, Albert Micajah (June 15, 1819—June 27, 1887)

Born in Stokes County, North Carolina; died in Cleveland Springs, North Carolina. Was graduated from the University of North Carolina in 1840. Admitted on trial to the South Carolina Conference of Methodist Episcopal Churches in 1841, and was ordained a deacon in 1843 and an elder in 1844. Was president of Greensboro Female College from 1848 to 1849. Was professor of history at the University of North Carolina from 1849 to 1859. Was professor of theology at Vanderbilt University from 1875 to 1885. Was the author of *The History of Methodism in South Carolina*.

SIMS, Thetis W. (April 25, 1852—December 17, 1939)

Born in Wayne County, Tennessee; died in Lexington, Tennessee. Was educated at Savannah (Tennessee) College; received his LL.B. from Cumberland University in 1876. Practiced law in Linden, Tennessee, beginning in 1876. Served in the United States House of Representatives from 1897 to 1921.

SMITH, Bessie (April 15, 1894—September 26, 1937)

Born in Chattanooga, Tennessee; died in Clarksdale, Mississippi. Was the daughter of a part-time Baptist preacher. At age nine she earned $8.00 for appearing in a Chattanooga theater. Played throughout the South and

Jim Farrell from Crutchfield: *Footprints*

developed a voice associated with the "Blues" movement. In 1923 she signed a contract with Columbia Records. Was termed the "Greatest Blues Singer in the World." Was killed in an automobile accident.

SMITH, Daniel (October 1748—June 1818)

Born in Stafford County, Virginia; died in Sumner County, Tennessee; buried in Sumner County. Attended William and Mary College. Was a surveyor; worked on the Virginia-North Carolina boundary line in 1779. Moved to the Cumberland River settlements in Tennessee in 1783. Was a trustee of Davidson Academy in 1785. Was brigadier general of the Mero District Militia in 1788. Was appointed secretary of the Southwest Territory in 1790. Drew the first map in 1794 of the area which became Tennessee two years later. Served in the United States Senate from 1798 to 1799 and from 1805 to 1809. Was the author of *A Short Description of the Tennessee Government*, published in 1793.

SMITH, Edmund Kirby (May 16, 1824—March 28, 1893)

Miller: *Photographic History of the Civil War*

Born in St. Augustine, Florida; died in Sewanee, Tennessee. Was graduated from the United States Military Academy in 1845. Served in the Mexican War. Taught math at the United States Military Academy from 1849 to 1852. Was appointed a lieutenant colonel of cavalry in the Confederate Army in 1861. Rose through the ranks until 1862 when he was promoted to lieutenant general. Placed in charge of the Trans-Mississippi department in 1863. Became full general in 1864 and was the last Confederate general to surrender. Was president of the University of Nashville from 1870 to 1875. Was professor of math at the University of the South from 1875 to 1893. Was the last surviving full general of either the United States or the Confederate Army.

SMITH, Elisabeth Howell (1854—?)

Born in Clarksville, Tennessee. Attended schools in Clarksville, Tennessee, then Bethel Female College in Kentucky. Was a suffragist who wrote numerous articles relating to women's suffrage. Was the author of *Desultory Tales of Colorado*.

SMITH, Henry G. (June 1807—December 31, 1878)

Born in Hartford, Connecticut; died in Memphis, Tennessee. Was an educator in North Carolina and Maryland. After his removal to Tennessee, he served on the Tennessee Supreme Court from 1867 to 1870.

SMITH, Samuel Axley (June 26, 1822—November 25, 1863)

Born in Monroe County, Tennessee; died in Polk County, Tennessee; buried in Polk County. Studied law; taught school; admitted to the Tennessee bar in 1845. Practiced law in Cleveland, Tennessee. Was district attorney general from 1845 to 1850. Served in the United States House of Representatives from 1853 to 1859. Was commissioner of the General Land Office, appointed by President Buchanan in 1860.

SMITH, William Ruthven (April 1868—July 15, 1941)

Born in Nashville, Tennessee; died in Sewanee, Tennessee. Attended Vanderbilt University; was graduated from the United States Military Academy in 1892. Rose in ranks in the United States Army from second lieutenant in 1892 to major general in 1924. Taught at the United States Military Academy for 11 years. Was commanding general of the Hawaiian Division from 1925 to 1927. Was superintendent of the United States Military Academy from 1928 to 1932. Became the superintendent of Sewanee Military Academy in 1932.

SMITHSON, Noble (December 7, 1841—?)

Born in Nolensville, Tennessee; died in Knoxville, Tennessee. Was self-educated; taught school in the country. Was admitted to the Tennessee bar in 1866; practiced law at Pulaski, Tennessee, from 1867 to 1887. Was attorney general of Tennessee from 1867 to 1869. Served in the Tennessee Senate from 1873 to 1874. Moved to Alabama and practiced law in Birmingham from 1888 to 1893. Moved to Knoxville, Tennessee, in 1893 and opened law practice there. Was the author of *Treatise on Civil Procedure in Tennessee*.

SNEED, John L. T. (1820—1901)

Born in Raleigh, North Carolina. Was a captain in the Mexican War and a brigadier general in the Confederacy. Served as a judge of the Tennessee Supreme Court from 1870 to 1878. Afterward, served as chancellor of the Shelby County (Tennessee) Chancery Court.

SNEED, William Henry (August 27, 1812—September 18, 1869)

Born in Davidson County, Tennessee; died in Knoxville, Tennessee; buried in Knoxville. Studied law and was admitted to the Tennessee bar in 1834; practiced in Murfreesboro, Tennessee. Served in the Tennessee Senate from 1843 to 1845. Moved to Knoxville, Tennessee, in 1845; practiced law there. Served in the United States House of Representatives from 1855 to 1857.

SNODGRASS, Charles Edward (?—?)

Born in Sparta, Tennessee; died in Tennessee. Moved to Crossville, Tennessee, and practiced law there. Was a member of the United States House of Representatives from 1889 to 1903.

SNODGRASS, David L. (April 4, 1851—October 11, 1917)

Born in Sparta, Tennessee. Was elected to the Tennessee House of Representatives in 1879. Was appointed to the Court of Referees in 1883. Was a judge on the Tennessee Supreme Court from 1886 to 1902; became chief justice in 1894.

SOULE, Joshua (August 1, 1781—March 6, 1867)

Born in Bristol, Maine; died in Nashville, Tennessee; buried in Nashville. Was admitted on trial to the New England Methodist Episcopal Conference in 1799. Was ordained an elder in 1802. Was a minister in New England from 1803 to 1816. Preached in churches in New York, Baltimore Conferences. Became a bishop assigned to the Western and Southern Conference in 1824 and served until 1844. Was senior bishop of the Southern Branch of the Methodist Episcopal Church in 1846. Soule is buried on the campus of Vanderbilt University.

SPENCER, Thomas Sharpe (?—April 1, 1794)

Died near Crab Orchard, Tennessee. Came to the Cumberland River Valley of Tennessee as early at 1776 and built cabins west of Bledsoe's Creek in what later became Sumner County. Cleared ground and planted corn in 1778, the first crop to be raised in Middle Tennessee. Spent one winter in a hollow sycamore tree near Bledsoe's Lick. Was famed as a hunter, explorer, and scout. Was killed by Indians near the headwaters of the Caney Fork River.

STAHLMAN, Edward Bushrod (September 2, 1843—August 12, 1930)

Born in Mecklenburg, Germany; died in Nashville, Tennessee. Moved to the United States in 1854. Was president of the city council of Nashville from 1875 to 1878. Served as vice-president of the Louisville and Nashville Railroad from 1885 to 1890. Became president of the *Nashville Banner* in 1885.

STANDIFER, James (?—August 20, 1837)

Born near Dunlap, Tennessee; died near Kingston, Tennessee; buried in Kingston. Was graduated from the University of Tennessee. Served in the United States House of Representatives from 1823 to 1825 and from 1829 to 1837.

STANTON, Frederick Perry (December 22, 1814—June 4, 1894)

Born in Alexandria, Virginia; died near Ocala, Florida; buried in South Lake Weir, Florida. Was graduated from George Washington University in 1833. Was admitted to the bar in Memphis, Tennessee. Contributed political articles to Memphis newspapers. Served in the United States House of Representatives from 1845 to 1855. Was appointed secretary of the Kansas Territory by President Buchanan in 1857. Became acting governor in 1858. Practiced law in Washington, D.C., from 1862.

STEARNS, Eben Sperry (December 23, 1819—April 11, 1887)

Born in Bedford, Massachusetts; died in Nashville, Tennessee. Was principal of Newburyport (Massachusetts) Female High School from 1846 to 1849 and of the Albany Female Academy from 1855 to 1869. Became the first president of the State Normal School in Nashville in 1875. Was chancellor of the University of Nashville from 1875 to 1887.

STEELE, William Owen (1918—June 25, 1979)

Born in Franklin, Tennessee; died in Chattanooga, Tennessee. Was graduated from Franklin (Tennessee) High School in 1936; from Cumberland University in Lebanon, Tennessee, in 1940. Was a World War II veteran, serving in the United States Army. Was an internationally known author of children's books who had written over 40 books, mostly with regional historical themes. His books won many awards, including the William Allen White Children's Book Award and the Thomas Alva Edison Award. Among his writings were *Flaming Arrows, The Buffalo Knife*, and *The Old Wilderness Road*.

STEWART, Alexander P. (October 2, 1821—1908)

Miller: *Photographic History of the Civil War*

Born in Rogersville, Tennessee. Attended schools in Tennessee. Was graduated from the United States Military Academy in 1842 and taught mathematics there in 1843. Was professor of mathematics and philosophy at Cumberland University and the University of Nashville from 1845 to 1860. Was commissioned a brigadier general in the Confederate Army in 1861. By 1864 he had attained the rank of lieutenant general. Had command of the Army of Tennessee at the war's end. Was chancellor of the University of Mississippi from 1874 to 1886. Assisted in the establishment of Chickamauga National Military Park in 1890.

STOKES, William B. (September 9, 1814—March 14, 1897)

Born in Chatham County, North Carolina; died in Alexandria, Tennessee; buried in Alexandria. Attended common schools; moved to Tennessee. Served in the Tennessee House of Representatives from 1849 to 1852. Served in the Tennessee Senate from 1855 to 1856. Was a member of the United States House of Representatives from 1859 to 1861 and from 1866 to 1871. Served in the United States Army during the War Between the States. Practiced law in Alexandria, Tennessee, after the war.

STONE, William (January 26, 1791—February 18, 1853)

Born in Sevier County, Tennessee; died in Sequatchie County, Tennessee. Was a captain in the Creek War; promoted to brigadier general for gallantry at Horseshoe Bend. Fought with Andrew Jackson at New Orleans. Was presented a cane by the United States Congress for his bravery at Tippecanoe. Served in the United States House of Representatives from 1837 to 1839.

STRIBLING, Thomas Sigismund "T. S." (May 4, 1881—July 8, 1965)

Born in Clifton, Tennessee; died in Clifton; buried in Clifton. Was graduated from the Normal College in Florence, Alabama, in 1903; from the University of Alabama 1904. Was instructor in novel writing at Columbia University. Was the author of many novels, including *Birthright* and *The Stone*, the latter a Pulitzer Prize winner.

STRICKLAND, William (1787—April 6, 1854)

Born in Philadelphia, Pennsylvania; died in Nashville, Tennessee; buried in Nashville. Was the noted architect who designed the Masonic Temple in Philadelphia in 1810, the first customs house in the United States in Philadelphia in 1819, and the Bank of the United States in 1824. He was brought to Nashville, Tennessee, in 1845 to implement his plans for the State Capitol and remained in Nashville for the rest of his life. Designed several Nashville public and private buildings. Strickland is interred in the north portico of the capitol building.

Gilchrist: *William Strickland; Architect and Engineer*

SUGG, William Daniel (July 16, 1897—December 5, 1981)

Born in Williamson County, Tennessee; died in Bradenton, Florida; buried in Bradenton. Was graduated from Battle Ground Academy in Franklin, Tennessee, and from Vanderbilt University in Nashville. Was a World War I veteran. Was graduated from Vanderbilt Medical School; practiced in eastern Kentucky for two years. Was a ship's doctor for a shipping line to Venezuela. Moved to Florida in 1930; was the only totally practicing surgeon between Miami and Tampa. Was the founder and president of the South Florida Museum. Was the originator of the Hernando De Soto celebration. Donated *Carnton*, the home of Randal McGavock, to a non-profit organization in his native Williamson County, Tennessee, to be preserved as a museum house.

SUMMERS, Thomas Osmond (October 11, 1812—May 6, 1882)

Born in Dorsetshire, England; died in Nashville, Tennessee. Came to the United States in 1830. Was admitted to the Baltimore Conference of the

Methodist Church in 1835; became an elder in 1839. Was a missionary in Houston and Galveston, Texas, from 1840 to 1844. Was the editor of the *Christian Advocate* in Nashville, Tennessee, from 1868 to 1878. Was professor of theology at Vanderbilt University from 1875 to 1882.

SUTHERLAND, Earl Wilbur (November 19, 1915—May 1974)

Born in Burlingame, Kansas. Became professor of physiology at Vanderbilt University School of Medicine in 1963. While at Vanderbilt, was the recipient of the Nobel Prize for Medicine for his work in hormone research (1971).

SWANN, Thomas Burnett (October 12, 1928—May 5, 1976)

Bill Potthast; Courtesy of Margaret Gaines Swann

Born in Tampa, Florida; buried in Winter Haven, Florida. Fantasy fiction author, poet, and critic. Swann spent summers as a youth in Tennessee; in 1955 he received his M.A. from the University of Tennessee at Knoxville, and in the early 1970s he returned to Knoxville to write. He was also an English professor in Florida. He wrote critical studies of poets Ernest Dowson and Christina Rossetti, four books of verse, and close to two dozen fantasy novels, often based on mythology. *The Day of the Minotaur* (1966) won a "Hugo" science-fiction award nomination; *How Are the Mighty Fallen* (1974) was the most critically acclaimed; all of his work displays polish, exoticism, and whimsy.

SWIGGART, William Harris, Jr. (October 12, 1888—October 30, 1966)

Born in Union City, Tennessee; died in Nashville, Tennessee. Was graduated from Vanderbilt University in 1910; received his LL.B. from Cumberland University in 1911; performed post-graduate work at the University of Michigan. Was admitted to the Tennessee bar in 1911; began a law practice at Union City, Tennessee. Was assistant attorney general for Tennessee from 1914 to 1926. Was a judge of the Tennessee Supreme Court from 1926 to 1935. Was general counsel for the Atlantic Coast Line Railroad from 1955 to 1956 and was a trustee for Vanderbilt University.

TATHAM, William (April 13, 1752—February 22, 1819)

Born in County Cumberland, England; died in Richmond, Virginia. Was clerk of the Watauga Association, the first permanent settlement in the region to become Tennessee. Drafted the petition for the inhabitants to be incorporated into North Carolina in 1776. Was admitted to the North Carolina bar in 1784; was a delegate to the North Carolina Assembly in 1787. Surveyed the United States coast from Cape Fear to Cape Hatteras from 1805 to 1810. Was the first citizen to defend the function of a national library for the United States. Was geographer of the United States State Department from 1810 to 1815 and was the author of *Memorial on the Civil and Military Government of the Tennessee Colony.*

TATUM, Howell (?—October 1822)

Born in Halifax County, North Carolina; died in Davidson County, Tennessee. Served in both the Revolution, under Washington, and the War of 1812, under Jackson. In 1796 was elected attorney general of the Mero District in Tennessee. A year later he became a judge on the Tennessee Superior Court and was later succeeded by Andrew Jackson.

TAYLOR, Alfred A. (August 6, 1848—November 1931)

Born in Cannon County, Tennessee; buried in Johnson City, Tennessee. Alfred Taylor was the older brother of former Tennessee Governor Robert Love Taylor, against whom he ran for the governor's chair in 1887. Was a lawyer by profession. Served in the United States House of Representatives before becoming governor of Tennessee himself in 1921.

Tennessee State Museum

TAYLOR, Nathaniel Green (December 29, 1819—April 1, 1887)

Born in Happy Valley, Tennessee; died in Happy Valley; buried in Happy Valley. Attended Washington College near Jonesboro, Tennessee. Was graduated from Princeton in 1840. Studied law; was admitted to the Tennessee bar in 1841; opened law practice in Elizabethton, Tennessee. Served in the United States House of Representatives from 1854 to 1855 and from 1866 to 1867. Was United States commissioner of Indian affairs from 1867 to

1869. Afterwards, became a farmer and minister. Was the father of Tennessee governors Alfred and Robert Love Taylor.

TAYLOR, Robert Love (July 31, 1850—March 31, 1912)

Tennessee State Museum

Born in Carter County, Tennessee; died in Washington, D.C.; buried in Johnson City, Tennessee. Was a newspaper editor, a lawyer, and an orator. Was a United States Representative in Congress at an early age. Defeated his brother, Alf, for the governorship of Tennessee in 1887. Served as governor until 1891. Served as governor again from 1897 to 1899. Afterwards, was elected to the United States Senate.

TEMPLE, Oliver Perry (January 27, 1820—1907)

Born in Greene County, Tennessee; died in Knoxville, Tennessee. Was admitted to the Tennessee bar in 1846. Moved to Knoxville, Tennessee, in 1848. Was appointed in 1850 by President Fillmore to membership of a committee to visit western Indian tribes. Was a Unionist during the War Between the States. Was postmaster of Knoxville from 1881 to 1885. Was a trustee of the University of Tennessee for forty years. Was the author of *East Tennessee and the Civil War*.

THOMAS, Cyrus (July 27, 1825—1910)

Dictionary of American Portraits

Born in Kingsport, Tennessee. Practiced law until 1865. Was county clerk of Jackson County, Illinois, from 1850 to 1853. Performed duties as an assistant on a geological survey from 1869 to 1873. Was professor of natural science at Southern Illinois University from 1873 to 1875. Became Illinois State Entomologist in 1874 and served until 1876. Was an archaeologist for the Bureau of American Ethnology from 1882 until his death. Was the author of many articles relative to the American Indians and moundbuilders.

THOMAS, Isaac (November 4, 1784—February 2, 1859)

Born in Sevierville, Tennessee; died in Alexandria, Louisiana; buried in Pineville, Louisiana. Was admitted to the Tennessee bar in 1808; began practice of law in Winchester, Tennessee. Served in the United States House of Representatives from 1815 to 1817. Moved to Alexandria, Louisiana, in 1819; practiced law and became one of the largest landowners and slave holders in Louisiana. Was the first man to introduce cultivated sugar cane into central Louisiana. Served in the Louisiana Senate from 1823 to 1827.

THOMAS, James Houston (September 22, 1808—August 4, 1876)

Born in Iredell County, North Carolina; died near Fayetteville, Tennessee; buried in Maury County, Tennessee. Was graduated from Jackson College in Columbia, Tennessee, in 1830. Was admitted to the Tennessee bar in 1831; practiced law in Columbia. Was attorney general of Tennessee from 1836 to 1842. Served in the United States House of Representatives from 1847 to 1851 and from 1859 to 1861.

THOMPSON, Jacob (May 15, 1810—March 24, 1885)

Born in Leasburg, North Carolina; died in Memphis, Tennessee; buried in Memphis. Was graduated from the University of North Carolina in 1831; was admitted to the North Carolina bar in 1834. Served in the United States House of Representatives from Mississippi from 1839 to 1851. Was secretary of the United States Department of the Interior from 1857 to 1861. Served in the Confederate Army. Was charged with complicity in Abraham Lincoln's assassination. Lived in Canada and Europe until 1868, when he returned to Oxford, Mississippi.

THORNBURGH, Jacob Montgomery (July 3, 1837—September 19, 1890)

Born in Tennessee; died in Knoxville, Tennessee; buried in Knoxville. Was admitted to the Tennessee bar in 1861; began law practice in Jefferson County, Tennessee. Served in the Tennessee Volunteer Cavalry of the United States Army. Was promoted through the ranks from private to lieutenant colonel from 1861 to 1863. After the war, resumed practice in Jefferson County. Moved to Knoxville, Tennessee, in 1867. Was attorney general for the Third Judicial Circuit Court of Tennessee. Was United States Commissioner at the International Exposition in Vienna in 1872. Served in the United States House of Representatives from 1873 to 1879.

THRUSTON, Gates Phillips (June 11, 1835—December 9, 1912)

Born in Dayton, Ohio; died in Nashville, Tennessee; buried in Nashville. Was judge advocate in the United States Army during the War Between the States. Served at Stones River and at Chickamauga. Settled in Nashville, Tennessee, in 1865. Was vice-president of the Tennessee Historical Society; was president of the Society of the Army of the Cumberland. Was an avid archaeologist. Wrote the book *Antiquities of Tennessee and Adjacent States* in 1890.

TILLMAN, LEWIS (August 18, 1816—May 3, 1886)

Born near Shelbyville, Tennessee; died in Shelbyville; buried in Shelbyville. Attended common schools. Was a Seminole War veteran. Served as clerk of the Bedford County Court from 1852 to 1860. Was master of the Chancery Court from 1865 to 1869. Served in the United States House of Representatives from 1869 to 1871.

TIMOTHY, Patrick H. (1897—October 27, 1981)

Born in Nashville, Tennessee; died in New Orleans, Louisiana; buried in Nashville. Was graduated from Duncan School in Nashville and attended Vanderbilt University for one year. Was graduated from the United States Military Academy in 1918. Served on active duty until 1946. Served in the Phillipine Islands and at West Point as an engineering instructor. Was district engineer for the United States Army Corps of Engineers in Chattanooga, Tennessee, and in New Orleans. Commanded 160,000 United States engineers under General Omar Bradley in World War II. Was the winner of the Distinguished Service Medal and the French Legion of Merit.

TIPTON, John (August 15, 1730—August 1813)

Born in Baltimore County, Maryland; died at Sinking Creek, North Carolina. Was a member of the Virginia House of Burgesses from 1774 to 1781. Served as a lieutenant colonel in the Virginia Militia. Was sheriff of Shenandoah County, Virginia, during the Revolution. Was elected to the North Carolina Assembly in 1785 in opposition to John Sevier, who was his arch-rival during the "lost" State of Franklin days. Was the representative from Washington County in the First Tennessee Assembly. Assisted in the drafting of the Tennessee Constitution in 1796. Served as a Tennessee state senator.

TIPTON, John (August 14, 1786—April 5, 1839)

Born in Sevier County, Tennessee; died in Logansport, Indiana; buried in Logansport. Served in the United States Army in the Tippecanoe campaign. Was promoted to brigadier general of the Indiana Militia in 1811; major general in 1822. Was the surveyor of the Indiana—Illinois border in 1821. Served in the United States Senate from Indiana from 1832 to 1839.

TOTTEN, Archibald W. O. (November 25, 1809—1867)

Born in Overton County, Tennessee. Served as a judge on the Tennessee Supreme Court from 1850 to 1855, when he resumed his law practice in Jackson, Tennessee. Was one of three commissioners appointed by Tennessee Governor Isham G. Harris to investigate the state's association with other southern states for the purpose of forming a defense pact.

TRIMBLE, John (February 7, 1812—February 23, 1884)

Born in Roane County, Tennessee; died in Nashville, Tennessee. Attended the University of Nashville. Was admitted to the Tennessee bar and practiced law in Nashville. Was attorney general of Tennessee from 1836 to 1842. Served in the Tennessee House of Representatives from 1843 to 1844; in the Tennessee Senate from 1845 to 1846, 1859, 1861, and from 1865 to 1867. Was United States attorney from 1862 to 1864. Served in the United States House of Representatives from 1867 to 1869.

TROOST, Gerard (March 15, 1776—August 14, 1850)

Born in Bois-Le-Duc, Holland; died in Nashville, Tennessee; buried in Nashville. Received an M.D. from the University of Leyden and a master of pharmacy degree from the University of Amsterdam. Was a member of a Dutch scientific commission to Java in 1809. Arrived in Philadelphia in 1810. Maintained a chemistry laboratory in Philadelphia from 1812 to 1817. Was professor of mineralogy at the Philadelphia Museum in 1821. Moved to Nashville, Tennessee, and served as professor of mineralogy and chemistry at the University of Nashville from 1828 to 1850. Was Tennessee State Geologist from 1831 to 1850.

TROUSDALE, William (1790—March 27, 1872)

Born in Orange County, North Carolina; buried in Gallatin, Tennessee. Was known as the "War Horse of Sumner County." Fought in the Creek War, the War of 1812, and the Mexican War. Was governor of Tennessee from 1849 to 1851. Afterwards was appointed to the post of United States minister to Brazil by President Franklin Pierce.

TURLEY, William Bruce (1800—May 27, 1851)

Born in Alexandria, Virginia; died in Shelby County, Tennessee. Was a judge of the Tennessee Supreme Court from 1835 to 1850. Was killed in a freak accident when part of his shattered walking stick pierced his body while he was attempting to regain his balance after a fall.

Green: Lives of the Judges of the Supreme Court of Tennessee

TURNEY, Hopkins Lacy (October 3, 1797—August 1, 1857)

Born in Dixon Springs, Tennessee; died in Winchester, Tennessee; buried in Winchester. Was apprenticed to a tailor as a young man; studied law. Was a Seminole War Veteran. Was admitted to the Tennessee bar and practiced law in Jasper and Winchester, Tennessee. Served in the Tennessee House of Representatives from 1825 to 1831, and from 1835 to 1837. Served in the United States House of Representatives from 1837 to 1843. Was a member of the United States Senate from 1845 to 1851.

TURNEY, Peter (September 22, 1827—1903)

Born in Jasper, Tennessee; died in Winchester, Tennessee. Was educated at private and public schools. Was admitted to the Tennessee bar in 1848; practiced at Winchester, Tennessee. Commanded Turney's First Tennessee Regiment during the War Between the States. Served on the Tennessee Supreme Court from 1870 to 1893; was chief justice from 1886 to 1893. Was governor of Tennessee from 1893 to 1897.

TYSON, Lawrence D. (July 4, 1861—August 24, 1929)

Born in Greeneville, North Carolina; died in Knoxville, Tennessee; buried in Knoxville. Was graduated from the United States Military Academy in 1883; received LL.B. from the University of Tennessee. Was admitted to the Tennessee bar in 1895. Was appointed by President McKinley as a colonel in the Sixth United States Volunteer Infantry in 1898. Served in the Spanish-American War. Was a brigadier general and the inspector general on the Tennessee governor's staff from 1902 to 1906. Served in the United States Senate from 1925 to 1931. Was a general in World War I; was winner of the Distinguished Service Medal.

V

VAUGHAN, William Wirt (July 2, 1831—August 19, 1878)

Born in LaGuardo, Tennessee; died in Crockett Mills, Tennessee; buried in Brownsville, Tennessee. Was graduated from Cumberland University at Lebanon, Tennessee. Studied law; was admitted to the Tennessee bar; practiced law at Brownsville, Tennessee. Served in the United States House of Representatives from 1871 to 1873. Was president of the Chesapeake and Ohio Railroad. Died suddenly while campaigning for election to the Forty-sixth Congress.

W

WADDELL, John Newton (April 2, 1812—January 9, 1895)

Born in Willington, South Carolina; died in Birmingham, Alabama. Was graduated from Franklin College in Georgia. Established Montrose Academy in Mississippi in 1842. Was ordained to the Presbyterian ministry in 1843. Was a founder of the University of Mississippi. Taught ancient languages at Presbyterian Synodical College at La Grange, Tennessee, from 1857 to 1860; was president from 1860 to 1862. Was a chaplain in the Confederate Army. Became chancellor of the University of Mississippi in 1865 and served until 1874. Was chancellor of Southwestern Presbyterian University at Clarksville, Tennessee, from 1879 to 1888.

WALKER, Joseph Rutherford (December 13, 1798—October 27, 1876)

Born in Roane County, Tennessee; died in California; buried in California. Was a trapper and trader working out of Independence, Missouri. Was sheriff of Jackson County, Missouri. Was a trapper and guide to the Rocky Mountains from 1832 to 1847. Was the first white man to cross the Sierra Mountains from the east. Was a discoverer of Yosemite Valley. Lived with the Shoshoni Indians. Discovered the pass through the mountains to California, which is named Walker Pass in his honor.

WALKER, Thomas (January 25, 1715—November 9, 1794)

Born in King and Queen County, Virginia; died in Albemarle County, Virginia. Was a physician by profession. Became the chief agent for the Loyal Company, a land speculation organization, in 1749. Served in the Virginia House of Burgesses in 1752 and from 1756 to 1761. Scouted out the "western" country for the Loyal Company and discovered the Cumberland Gap and the Cumberland River in Tennessee.

WALKER, William (May 8, 1824—September 12, 1860)

Carr: The World and William Walker

Born in Nashville, Tennessee; died in Trujillo, Honduras; buried in Trujillo. Was one of the youngest men to be graduated from the University of Nashville (1838). Received an M.D. degree from the University of Pennsylvania in 1843. Studied in Edinburgh, Scotland. Became a lawyer but was dissatisfied with the profession. Left Nashville and became a newspaperman in New Orleans in 1848. Went to California in 1850. At the head of a small army, he proclaimed Lower California as an independent republic with himself as president, in 1853. Invaded Nicaragua and was elected its president in 1856. Was executed in Honduras. Was the author of *The War in Nicaragua.*

WALLACE, Nathaniel Dick (October 27, 1845—July 16, 1894)

Born in Columbia, Tennessee; died in Asheville, North Carolina; buried in New Orleans, Louisiana. Was graduated from Trinity College in Dublin, Ireland, in 1865. Was president of the New Orleans Produce Exchange. Served in the United States House of Representatives from Louisiana from 1886 to 1887.

WARD, Nancy (1738—1824)

Born in the Cherokee village of Chota in Tennessee; died on the Ocoee River, Tennessee. Was an important Cherokee woman who was given the title "Beloved Woman" by her tribe for her role in turning the tide against the Creek enemy in the Battle of Taliwa in 1755. Later she saved the white settlement at Watauga by warning the inhabitants of an imminent attack by the pro-British Cherokees. In her closing years she operated an inn on the Ocoee River in East Tennessee.

WARNER, James Cartwright (August 30, 1830—July 21, 1895)

Born in Gallatin, Tennessee. Established a hardware business in Chattanooga, Tennessee, in 1852. Served as mayor of Chattanooga and in the Tennessee legislature. Spent 25 years in developing the mineral resources of the South. Was president of the Tennessee Coal, Iron, and Railroad Company from 1874 to 1898. Was organizer of the Warner Iron Company and its president from 1880 to 1889. His "Warner furnace" was the leader in the charcoal iron industry.

WATKINS, Albert G. (May 5, 1818—November 9, 1895)

Born near Jefferson City, Tennessee; died in Mooresburg, Tennessee; buried in Jefferson City. Was graduated from Holston College in Tennessee. Was admitted to the Tennessee bar and began a law practice in Panther Springs, Tennessee, in 1839. Served in the Tennessee House of Representatives in 1845; in the United States House of Representatives from 1849 to 1853 and from 1855 to 1859.

WATTERSON, Harvey Magee (November 23, 1811—October 1, 1891)

Born in Beech Grove, Tennessee; died in Louisville, Kentucky; buried in Louisville. Attended Cumberland College in Kentucky. Established and edited a newspaper in Shelbyville, Tennessee. Was admitted to the Tennessee bar. Served in the Tennessee House of Representatives from 1831 to 1839; in the United States House of Representatives from 1839 to 1843. Was presiding officer of the Tennessee Senate from 1845 to 1847. Owned the *Nashville Daily Union* in 1849; was its editor from 1850 to 1851. Later became a member of the editorial staff of the *Courier Journal* in Louisville, Kentucky.

WEAKLEY, Robert (July 20, 1764—February 4, 1845)

Born in Halifax County, Virginia; died in Nashville, Tennessee; buried in Nashville. Attended school in Princeton, New Jersey. Was a Revolutionary War veteran. Farmed in that part of North Carolina which became the state of Tennessee. Was a member of the North Carolina convention which ratified the United States Constitution in 1789. Served in the first Tennessee House of Representatives in 1796; in the United States House of Representatives from 1809 to 1811. Was the United States commissioner to treaty with the Chickasaws in 1819. Attended the Tennessee Constitutional Convention in 1834.

WHARTON, Jesse (July 29, 1782—July 22, 1833)

Born in Albemarle County, Virginia; died in Nashville, Tennessee; buried in Nashville. Was admitted to the Virginia bar and practiced in Albemarle

County. Moved to Tennessee where he served in the United States House of Representatives from 1807 to 1809; in the United States Senate from 1814 to 1815. Was a member of the board of visitors at the United States Military Academy in 1832.

WHITE, Alexander (October 16, 1816—December 13, 1893)

Born in Franklin, Tennessee; died in Dallas, Texas; buried in Dallas. Attended the University of Tennessee. Was a veteran of the Seminole War in 1836. Was admitted to the bar in 1838 and began practice in Talledega, Alabama. Served in the United States House of Representatives from Alabama from 1851 to 1853 and from 1873 to 1875. Served in the Alabama House of Representatives in 1872. Was an associate judge on the United States Court for Utah Territory in 1875. Moved to Dallas, Texas, in 1876 and practiced law.

WHITE, Edward Douglas (March 1795—April 18, 1847)

Born in Maury County, Tennessee; died in New Orleans, Louisiana; buried in Thibodaux, Louisiana. Was graduated from the University of Nashville in 1845. Practiced law in Donaldsonville, Tennessee. Was associate judge of the New Orleans City Court from 1825 to 1828. Served in the United States House of Representatives from Louisiana from 1829 to 1834 and from 1839 to 1843. Was governor of Louisiana from 1835 to 1839. Practiced law in Thibodaux from 1843 to 1847.

WHITE, Hugh Lawson (October 30, 1773—April 10, 1840)

Born in Iredell County, North Carolina; died in Knoxville, Tennessee; buried in Knoxville. Was the son of General James White, the founder of Knoxville. Was a judge on the Tennessee Superior Court from 1801 to 1807 and from 1809 to 1815. In 1825 was elected to fill Andrew Jackson's unexpired term in the United States Senate. Ran against Martin Van Buren in 1836 for the United States Presidency and gained considerable support from the South and West.

WHITE, James (1749—August 14, 1821)

Born in Rowan County, North Carolina; died in Knoxville, Tennessee; buried in Knoxville. Was a captain of the North Carolina Militia from 1779 to 1781. Settled the site of Knoxville, Tennessee, in 1786. Served in the North Carolina House of Commons in 1789. Was a member of the Tennessee Constitutional Convention in 1796. Was brigadier general of the Tennessee

Militia in 1798. Elected to the Tennessee Senate in 1796; was presiding officer in 1801 and 1803. Donated the site in Knoxville for the University of Tennessee.

WHITEHEAD, Don (1909—January 12, 1981)

Died in Knoxville, Tennessee. Was a two-time Pulitzer Prize winner for journalism. Was the author of *The FBI Story* and *Attack on Terror*. Worked in Memphis and Knoxville for the Associated Press. Was the winner of the United States Army's Medal of Freedom for his coverage of World War II.

WHITESIDE, Jenkins (1772—September 25, 1822)

Born in Lancaster, Pennsylvania; died in Nashville, Tennessee; buried in Nashville. Was admitted to the Pennsylvania bar. Moved to Tennessee and practiced law in Knoxville. Was commissioner of Knoxville from 1801 to 1802. Served in the United States Senate from 1809 to 1811.

WHITTHORNE, Washington Curran (April 19, 1825—September 21, 1891)

Born near Farmington, Tennessee; died in Columbia, Tennessee; buried in Columbia. Was graduated from the University of Tennessee in 1843. Was admitted to the Tennessee bar in 1845; began practice of law in Columbia. Served in the Tennessee Senate from 1855 to 1858. Was elected to the Tennessee House of Representatives in 1859; was speaker in 1859. Was adjutant general of the Tennessee Confederate Army from 1861 to 1865. Served in the United States House of Representatives from 1871 to 1883 and from 1887 to 1891. Served in the United States Senate from 1886 to 1887.

WHYTE, Robert (January 6, 1767—November 12, 1844)

Born in Wigtonshire, Scotland; died in Nashville, Tennessee. Taught languages at William and Mary College as a young man. Was appointed to the Tennessee Supreme Court of Errors and Appeals and served until 1834.

Green: *Lives of the Judges of the Supreme Court of Tennessee*

WILKES, John Summerville (March 2, 1841—February 2, 1908)

Born in Maury County, Tennessee. Served with Nathan Bedford Forrest at the Battle of Brice's Cross Roads. Practiced law in Pulaski, Tennessee. Was judge of the Tennessee Supreme Court from 1893 to 1908.

WILLIAMS, Hiram King "Hank" (September 17, 1923—January 1, 1953)

Born in Georgiana, Alabama; died in Oak Hill, Virginia; buried in Montgomery, Alabama. Sang in a church choir at age six. Won an amateur contest as a teenager, then played for the Louisiana Hayride. In 1949 he signed with the Grand Ole Opry and then produced a long line of top-selling records. Died on the way to a concert in Ohio. Elected to the Country Music Hall of Fame in 1961.

Les Leverett

WILLIAMS, James (July 1, 1796—April 10, 1869)

Born in Grainger County, Tennessee; died in Gratz, Austria; buried in Austria. Was the founder of the *Knoxville Post* in 1841. Served in the Tennessee House of Representatives in 1843. Was the founder of the Deaf and Dumb Asylum in Knoxville. Served as United States minister to Turkey from 1858 to 1860. Was the author of *Letters on Slavery from the Old World*.

WILLIAMS, John (January 29, 1778—August 10, 1837)

Born in Surry County, North Carolina; died in Knoxville, Tennessee. Was admitted to the Tennessee bar in 1803. Was a colonel in the Tennessee Volunteers from 1812 to 1814. Served in the United States Senate beginning in 1815. Was chairman of the committee on military affairs in the United States Senate from 1817 to 1823. Was United States charge d'affaires to the Federation of Central America in 1825. Was elected to the Tennessee Senate in 1827.

WILLIAMS, Joseph Lanier (October 23, 1810—December 14, 1865)

Born in Knoxville, Tennessee; died in Knoxville; buried in Knoxville. Attended the University of East Tennessee and the United States Military Academy. Was admitted to the Tennessee bar and practiced in Knoxville. Served in the

United States House of Representatives from 1837 to 1843. Practiced law in Washington, D.C. Was judge of the United States District Court for the Dakota Territory, appointed by President Lincoln.

WILLIAMS, Samuel Cole (January 15, 1864—December 14, 1947)

Green: Lives of the Judges of the Supreme Court of Tennessee

Born in Gibson County, Tennessee; died in Johnson City, Tennessee. Attended school in Humboldt, Tennessee. Was graduated from Vanderbilt University in 1884. Practiced law in Jonesboro, Tennessee. Served on the planning committee of the American Bar Association in 1913. Served on the Tennessee Supreme Court from 1913 to 1918. Was dean of the Lamar School of Law at Emory University from 1919 to 1924. Was a noted historian and writer of historical books and articles. Was author of *Early Travels in the Tennessee Country, History of the Lost State of Franklin,* and many others.

WILLIAMS, Thomas Lanier (?—?)

Born in North Carolina; died in Nashville, Tennessee. Was appointed to the Supreme Court of Errors and Appeals in 1826, but served less than one year since the number of judges was reduced from five to four. Was chancellor of the Chancery Court of Tennessee from 1836 to 1854.

WILLIAMS, Thomas Lanier "Tennessee" (March 26, 1914—February 12, 1983)

The Tennessean

Born in Columbus, Mississippi; died in New York City. Was a descendant of General James White, the founder of Knoxville, and of Valentine Sevier. Lived in Nashville, Tennessee, for two years around 1916. His grandfather was Walter E. Dakin, a graduate of the University of the South at Sewanee, Tennessee, and later a minister in South Pittsburg and Cleveland, Tennessee. He

167

adopted the name, "Tennessee," in 1939, after selling his first magazine story. In later years, he was most noted for his plays, *The Glass Menagerie, Cat on a Hot Tin Roof, Streetcar Named Desire,* and *Summer and Smoke.*

WINCHESTER, James (February 6, 1752—July 1826)

Born in Westminister, Maryland; died in Sumner County, Tennessee; buried in Sumner County. Served in the American Revolution; was wounded and captured on Staten Island in 1777. Was exchanged and captured again at Charleston in 1780. Moved to Tennessee in 1785, although at that time it was still a part of North Carolina. Was a member of the North Carolina Convention to ratify the United States Constitution. Was brigadier general of the Mero district. Was brigadier general in command of the Army of the Northwest during the War of 1812. Was one of the founders, along with Andrew Jackson and John Overton, of Memphis, Tennessee.

WINDOLPH, Charles (December 9, 1851—March 11, 1950)

Born in Bergen, Germany; buried in Black Hills National Cemetery, South Dakota. Windolph enlisted in H Troop, Seventh United States Cavalry, at Nashville, Tennessee, on July 23, 1872, under the alias of Charles Wrangle. In the fall of 1872 he took part in an expedition from Nashville to Livingston, Alabama, to guard the polls during the gubernatorial election. At the Battle of the Little Big Horn, Windolph won the Congressional Medal of Honor for protecting a water detail during the fighting on Reno's Hill, June 26, 1876. He was the last surviving member of the Seventh Cavalry who fought at the Little Big Horn. (See also BENTEEN, Frederick William.)

Custer Battlefield National Monument

WRIGHT, Archibald (1809—September 13, 1884)

Born in Maury County, Tennessee. Was a teacher, soldier in the Seminole War, a state legislator, and practicing attorney. Was a judge on the Tennessee Supreme Court from 1851 to 1861.

WRIGHT, Frances "Fanny" (September 6, 1795—December 13, 1852)

Born in Dundee, Scotland. Moved to New York in 1818. Was a playwright.

Went to England in 1820; returned to the United States in 1824. Was the organizer of Nashoba in Tennessee, a colony which experimented in the emancipation of slaves. Was the editor of the *New Harmony Gazette* in 1828. Afterwards was a social lecturer and writer.

WRIGHT, Luke E. (1846—November 17, 1922)

Born in Tennessee; died in Memphis, Tennesse. Was the son of Archibald Wright, a judge on the Tennessee Supreme Court. Practiced law in Memphis. Was attorney general of Tennessee for eight years. Was appointed civil governor of the Phillipine Islands in 1904; was governor general until 1906. Was United States ambassador to Japan from 1906 to 1907. Was United States secretary of war from 1908 to 1909 in the administration of Theodore Roosevelt.

Y

YANDELL, Lunsford Pitts (July 4, 1805—February 4, 1878)

Born near Hartsville, Tennessee; died in Louisville, Kentucky. Attended Transylvania University in Lexington, Kentucky. Was graduated from the University of Maryland at Baltimore in 1825. Practiced medicine at Murfreesboro, Tennessee, in 1826. Moved to Nashville, Tennessee, in 1830. Was professor of chemistry and pharmacy at Transylvania University from 1831 to 1837. Was an organizer of the Louisville, Kentucky, Medical Institute in 1837. Taught medicine at Memphis, Tennessee, until the War Between the States. Was a hospital surgeon in the Confederate Army. Was the author of *Contributions to the Geology of Kentucky*.

YELL, Archibald (August 1797—February 23, 1847)

Born in North Carolina; died in Mexico; buried in Fayetteville, Arkansas. Served in the Creek War and the War of 1812. Was admitted to the Tennessee bar and served in the Tennessee legislature. Was in charge of the United States land office in Little Rock, Arkansas, in 1831. Was territorial judge for Arkansas from 1832 to 1835. Served in the United States House of Representatives from Arkansas from 1836 to 1839 and from 1845 to 1846. Was governor of Arkansas from 1840 to 1844. Was killed at the Battle of Buena Vista.

YERGER, William (November 22, 1816—June 7, 1872)

Born in Lebanon, Tennessee. Was graduated from the University of Nashville in 1833. Was a member of the Tennessee bar. Was associate justice on the Mississippi Supreme Court from 1851 to 1853. Served in the Mississippi legislature from 1861 to 1865. Was a member of the Mississippi Constitutional Convention in 1865.

YOAKUM, Henderson (September 6, 1810—November 30, 1856)

Born in Powell's Valley, Tennessee; died in Houston, Texas. Was graduated from the United States Military Academy in 1832. Was a captain in the Murfreesboro Sentinels Company in 1833. Was a colonel in the Tennessee Infantry in 1838. Served in the Tennessee Senate from 1839 to 1845. Admitted to the Republic of Texas bar in 1845. Served in the Mexican War from 1845 to 1846. Yoakum County, Texas, is named in his honor. Was the author of *History of Texas from its First Settlement in 1685 to its Annexation to the United States in 1846.*

YOUNGER, Thomas Coleman (January 5, 1844—February 21, 1916)

Born in Lee's Summit, Missouri; died in Lee's Summit; buried in Lee's Summit. Younger probably came to Tennessee in the summer of 1875. Teaming up with Frank James (See JAMES, Alexander Franklin), he reportedly participated in the robbery of the Bank of Huntington, West Virginia, on September 6, 1875. In 1903, following his release from prison, Cole teamed up with Frank James again, this time in a Wild West show. The James-Younger Wild West Show, a seedy imitation of "Buffalo Bill's", toured the state in May and June. It was almost universally condemned by the press wherever it went and several members of the cast were jailed for assorted crimes during the tour. Younger and the show left Tennessee under a cloud.

Z

ZOLLICOFFER, Felix Kirk (May 19, 1812—June 19, 1862)

Harper's Pictorial History of the Civil War.

Born in Maury County, Tennessee; died in Kentucky; buried in Nashville, Tennessee. Attended Jackson College in Jackson, Tennessee. Fought in the Seminole War. Was editor of the *Nashville Republican Banner* in 1843. Was adjutant general and comptroller of Tennessee from 1845 to 1849. Served in the Tennessee Senate from 1849 to 1852; in the United States House of Representatives from 1853 to 1859. Was a brigadier general in command of East Tennessee during the War Between the States. Was killed in action.

SELECTED BIBLIOGRAPHY

Cisco, Jay Guy. *Historical Sumner County, Tennessee.* Nashville: Folk-Keelin, 1909. Reprinted Nashville: Charles Elder, 1971.

Crutchfield, James A. *Footprints Across the Pages of Tennessee History.* Nashville: Williams Press, 1976.

Davis, Louise Littleton. *More Tales of Tennessee.* Gretna, Louisiana: Pelican Publishing Company, 1978.

Dellar, Fred and Thompson, Roy. *The Illustrated Encyclopedia of Country Music.* New York: Harmony Books, 1977.

Durham, Walter T. *Old Sumner: A History of Sumner County, Tennessee from 1805 to 1861.* Gallatin, Tennessee: Sumner County Library, 1972.

Goodpasture, Albert V. "A Dictionary of Distinguished Tennesseans" in *The American Historical Magazine*, Vol. VIII, No. 2. Nashville: 1903.

Green, John W. *Lives of the Judges of the Supreme Court of Tennessee.* Knoxville: 1947.

McBride, Robert M. and Robison, Dan M. *Biographical Directory of the Tennessee General Assembly.* Vols. 1 & 2. Nashville: The State Library and Archives and the Tennessee Historical Commission, 1975, 1979.

Makers of Millions. Nashville: Tennessee Department of Agriculture, 1952.

Miller, Francis T. (Ed.) *The Photographic History of the Civil War.* Vol. 10. New York: The Review of Reviews Company, 1911.

Phillips, Margaret I. *The Governors of Tennessee.* Gretna, Louisiana: Pelican Publishing Company, 1978.

Who Was Who in America. Vols. 1-5. Chicago: Marquis—Who's Who, Inc., 1967, 1968.

Yeatman, Ted. P. *Jesse James and Bill Ryan at Nashville.* Ballads by Steve Eng. Nashville: Depot Press, 1981.

INDEX

This index consists of one entry per person included in the book. Naturally, some of those people appearing herein justly qualify to be listed in more than one category of the index; e.g., "Politics," "Military," and "Judicial." However, the author has attempted to place each name in that category in which posterity best remembers the person. It was a matter of judgement, and as the sole selector of the entries, the author alone exercised that judgement.

Boyd, Sempronius Hamilton, 27
Campbell, George Washington, 36
Cooper, Prentice, 48
Eaton, John Henry, 60
Evans, Henry C., 63
Gayoso De Lemos, Manuel, 73
Hull, Curdell, 88
Johnson, Cave, 94
Marling, John Leake, 110
Maynard, Horace, 111
Maynard, James, 112
Miro, Esteban Rodriguez, 115
Polk, William Hawkins, 129
Porter, James D., 129
Sevier, Ambrose Hundley, 145
Trousdale, William, 159
Williams, James, 166
Williams, John, 166
Wright, Luke E., 169

Hargrove, Robert Kennon, 80
Joynes, Edward Southey, 96
Kirkland, James Hampton, 98
Lindsley, John Berrien, 102
Lindsley, Phillip, 103
Link, Samuel Albert, 103
Lipscomb, David, 103
McAnally, David Rice, 105
McTyeire, Holland Nimmons, 109
Melton, Wrightman Fletcher, 113
Pearson, Josephine, 125
Priestley, James 131
Rose, Wickliffe, 139
Savage, George Martin, 142
Scott, William Anderson, 143
Shipp, Albert Micajah, 147
Stearns, Eben Sperry, 151
Waddell, John Newton, 161

EDUCATION

Atkinson, Thomas, 15
Baxter, Edmund Dillabunty, 19
Benton, Thomas Hart, 23
Braden, John, 28
Brown, Milton, 30
Campbell, Francis J., 36
Carrick, Samuel, 38
Claxton, Philander Priestley, 43
Cockrill, Ann Robertson, 45
Cooke, Richard Joseph, 47
Cravath, Erastus Milo, 50
Dabney, Charles Williams, 53
Donnell, Robert, 59
Fanning, Tolbert, 65
Fisk, Clinton Bowen, 65
Fitzpatrick, Morgan C., 66
Fowler, Joseph Smith, 69
Gailor, Thomas Frank, 71
Garland, Landon Cabell, 72
Gordon, George W., 76
Green, William Mercer, 77
Groves, James Robinson, 77

ENTERTAINMENT

Akeman, David "Stringbean," 10
Coggin, Barbara, 46
Cooper, Dale T. "Stoney," 48
Copas, Lloyd "Cowboy," 49
Flatt, Lester Raymond, 66
Foley, Clyde Julian "Red," 67
Handy, William Christopher
    "W. C.," 79
Hawkins, Harold "Hawkshaw,"
    83
Hay, George Dewey, 83
Hensley, Virginia Patterson "Patsy
    Cline," 85
Hesselberg, Melvyn Edward
    "Melvyn Douglas," 86
Hunter, William Randolph, 89
Lewis, Walter 'Furry," 101
Ludlow, Noah Miller, 104
Melton, James, 112
Moore, Grace, 117
Presley, Elvis Aaron, 130
Reeves, Jame Travis "Jim," 134
Ritter, Woodward Maurice "Tex,"

MILITARY

176

POLITICS

RELIGION

SCIENCE AND MEDICINE

MISCELLANEOUS

ABOUT THE AUTHOR

James A. Crutchfield is an award-winning historical writer who lives in Franklin, Tennessee. A native-born Tennessean, Crutchfield is descended from one of the first families to settle in Nashville. The author of eight books and numerous magazine articles, he is currently completing a book on the history of the Natchez Trace.

Crutchfield's published books include: *The Harpeth River: A Biography* (1972, 1973); *Early Times in The Cumberland Valley* (1975, 1976); *A Primer of Handicrafts of The Southern Appalachians* (1976); *Footprints Across the Pages of Tennessee History* (1976); *Williamson County: A Pictorial History* (1980); *Yesteryear in Nashville* (1981); and *A Heritage of Grandeur* (1981). He has published articles in: *Nashville Magazine, Tennessee Historical Quarterly, Early American Life, Cumberland Magazine, Tennessee Valley Historical Review, Williamson County Historical Society Review*, and *The Magazine Antiques.*

A designer and illustrator as well as an author, including the design and illustration of *Engineers on the Twin Rivers* for the U.S. Army Corps of Engineers, Crutchfield's published maps include: *A Bicentennial Map of Williamson County, A Map of the Prehistoric Cumberland Valley, Historic Hendersonville, Historic Goodlettsville, Historic Maury County, Historic Williamson County, Historic Dickson County, Historic Lewis County, A Chronology of Williamson County History*, and *A Bicentennial Map of Nashville.*

He is the editor for *Your Tennessee*, used in all Tennessee Public Schools and is past editor of the *Tennessee Valley Historical Review* and a writer for WSM-TV's Century III "Yesteryear in Nashville" Series. His *The Harpeth River: A Biography* won the 1973 Certificate of Commendation from the American Association for State and Local History, and his article, "Pioneer Architecture in Tennessee," published in the *Tennessee Historical Quarterly*, won the Tennessee American Revolutionary Bicentennial Commission's prize for best writing.

Active in history endeavors as well as its research and authorship, Crutchfield belongs to the Tennessee Historical Society; is past president of the Williamson County Historical Society, as well as the Pioneers' Corner, Inc.; and is a member of the Dickson County Historical Society and the National Trust for Historic Preservation.